Han

✔ KU-522-508

So you know Tere's
no place like home

Berlitz

BEN xx

London

January
2009

Front cover: Tower Bridge

Right: Big Ben

TOP 10 ATTRACTIONS

Tower of London • Where many an historic head has rolled *(page 69)*

Harrods • London's most famous corner shop, known for its exquisite Art Nouveau food hall *(page 71)*

Tate Modern • Feted for its architecture and its excellent collection of modern and contemporary art *(page 57)*

Big Ben • The clocktower dominates the Palace of Westminster, home of the Parliament *(page 32)*

The British Museum · Located in Bloomsbury, it houses artefacts from antiquity to the 20th century *(page 49)*

St Paul's Cathedral · Sir Christopher Wren's masterpiece is the jewel of the City *(page 66)*

Covent Garden · Named after its market, it's a lively area for shopping and street performance *(page 40)*

The National Gallery · Located in Trafalgar Square, it houses Britain's finest collection of European art *(page 24)*

The London Eye · Take a ride for spectacular views over London *(page 53)*

Buckingham Palace · Witness age-old traditions at the Queen's London residence *(page 29)*

CONTENTS

25

64

83

102

9

37

INTRODUCTION

London is a city steeped in history, with incredible archi-tectural richness, vast cultural offerings and great inter-national political, economic and religious influence. It is a cosmopolitan place, where, at best, a refreshingly open at-titude towards its many citizens and visitors of diverse eth-nic backgrounds can be felt. You can enjoy the food of most nations and cultures here, and there are pubs, bars and en-tertainment to suit all tastes. William Shakespeare could have been referring to his adopted hometown of London when he wrote, 'Age cannot wither her, nor custom stale her infinite variety.'

Yet London is not without its problems. The basic cost of living – from food prices to travel and rent – is sky high compared with that in most other capitals and, certainly, other cities in the UK. Despite the creaking public transport system costing its users dear, there are few days when jour-neys are not inconvenienced by signal failure or other age-old excuses. The great distances between boroughs mean that locals (and visitors) have to be prepared for long commutes or treks across town to reach their destination (a journey to and from work of anything up to an hour is considered per-fectly normal among London commuters).

The 'Big Smoke' has its major pollution concerns too, owing to traffic congestion, although this is certainly nothing new – in 1819 the poet Percy Bysshe Shelley wrote 'Hell is a city much like London, A populous and smoky city.' Thank-fully, though, the 'congestion charge' scheme, which taxes anyone taking a car through a defined central zone between 7am and 6pm from Monday to Friday, is beginning to ad-

The London Eye on the South Bank of the Thames

Scots Guard, Buckingham Palace

dress this problem by reducing the amount of traffic on the city's streets.

For many of those who come to visit or work in the capital, the pros obviously still outweigh the cons, as people flock here.

Population

After decades of decline, London's population has increased since the mid-1980s to its present 7.5 million, and forecasts show it surging to almost 8 million by 2016. Over one in three residents is from a minority ethnic group, and around 300 languages are spoken (from Abem, a language of the Ivory Coast, to Zulu, from South Africa). More than 250,000 refugees have come to London over the past 15 years, and higher percentage of Indians and Pakistanis now own their own homes in the capital than white people. Service industries such as catering and hospitals rely heavily on immigrant labour. Prosperity ranges from the billionaires of Belgravia to the down-and-outs sleeping rough in shop doorways.

The Climate

The climate in London is mild, with the warming effects of the city itself keeping off the worst of the cold in winter. Snow (other than a quick flurry) and temperatures below freezing are fairly unusual, with January temperatures averaging 43°F (6°C). Temperatures in the summer months average 64°F (18°C), but they can soar to well over 85°F (30°C), causing the city to become stiflingly hot (air-conditioning is not universal).

However, temperatures can fluctuate considerably from day to day, and surprise showers catch people unawares all year round. (This unpredictability has its plus side – Brits love to complain and converse about the weather.) Unsuspecting visitors should come prepared with wet-weather clothes, whatever the season; layers are sensible.

An Organic City

Take your time in London because there is no chance that you'll see it all. While the city has a long and venerable past, that past is often hidden from view. Over the centuries the ripples of history have repeatedly destroyed parts of the city, and the subsequent rebuilding has resulted in a cocktail of streets that combine many different styles.

When Queen Boudicca razed the city the Romans had built here in AD61, this was just the first of many setbacks London

London's City skyline by night: St Paul's and 'The Gherkin'

Hailing a black cab

was to experience. The plague of 1665 claimed the lives of over 110,000 Londoners, and in 1666 the Great Fire that began in Pudding Lane destroyed much of the city (although it claimed incredibly few victims). In the bombing blitz of World War II, 29,000 Londoners were killed, 80 percent of buildings in the City (the financial area) were damaged and a third were destroyed.

Yet throughout this process of change, some good seems to have come out of most disasters. So dark and narrow were the streets in the old City of London, for example,

London Cabbies

About 20,000 drivers work in London, half of them as owner-drivers. The others either hire vehicles from big fleets or work night shifts in someone else's cab. In all, there are more than 15,000 vehicles. The classic cab, the FX4, was launched in 1959 and some models are still going strong. The newer Metrocab is more spacious.

Would-be drivers must register with the Public Carriage Office and then spend up to four years learning London in minute detail (called 'doing the Knowledge'). They achieve this by travelling the streets of the metropolis on a moped, whatever the weather, working out a multitude of routes from a clipboard mounted on the handlebars. Even though the allegedly garrulous cabbies may not always know what they're talking about, they do know where they're going.

that shopkeepers had to erect mirrors outside their windows to reflect light into the shops. The bombing of World War II eventually provided the opportunity for widening and lightening; slums disappeared, and the level of street crime declined.

A City in Vogue

Every now and then the city becomes brazenly fashionable – the Swinging London of the 1960s, for instance, or 'the coolest place on the planet', as *Newsweek* dubbed it in the 1990s – but what attracts millions of visitors, year in and year out, is less the sparkling baubles of popular culture than the

Relaxing in Hyde Park, one of London's great green spaces

crown jewels of continuity and tradition. It's a patchy, unplanned city, and you never know what you are going to find around the next corner – gothic carvings adorning a Victorian office block, a narrow alley that has defied redevelopers for seven centuries, a blue plaque on the wall of an ordinary-looking house testifying that Benjamin Franklin, Florence Nightingale, Karl Marx or Jimi Hendrix once lived there, or even the pomp of a state occasion. Certainly, there is enough to keep even the most demanding of visitors and locals busy – as Dr Samuel Johnson famously declared, 'when a man is tired of London, he is tired of life; for there is in London all that life can afford.'

A BRIEF HISTORY

Although Julius Caesar, in his ever-expanding quest for empire, landed in England in 56 and 55BC, he came, he saw and he left without leaving any trace of a settlement. It remained for the Emperor Claudius and his Roman legions to conquer the island in AD43 and build what was believed to be the first bridge over the Thames (roughly on the site of today's London Bridge), establishing the trade port of Londinium.

The Romans built roads, forts, temples, villas, a basilica, forum and a huge amphitheatre (excavated near the Guildhall in 1988) for the population of around 50,000 in the area now known as the City. The Roman's rule was often challenged, and so they erected vast stone walls around their city.

Saxons and Normans

The Roman Empire began to decline, and the legions were recalled from London in 410. The walled area of Londonium became a ghost town, buried under silt and grass, as invaders avoided it. Eventually, the Saxons came over the North Sea to build Lundenwic, and, after a brief return to paganism, the seeds of Christianity sown by the late Romans sprouted in London again. St Ethelbert, the first Christian king, dedicated a small church to St Paul, which over the succeeding centuries was destroyed and rebuilt four times.

The Saxon kings were constantly at battle with Viking and Danish invaders, and when the Danes conquered and put King Canute on the throne in 1016, London unseated Winchester as the capital of the kingdom. In the 1040s Westminster Abbey was built by Edward the Confessor, a pious though ineffectual king. When the Norman army of William the Conqueror was victorious at the Battle of Hastings in 1066, William began the tradition of being crowned at the Abbey. He respected London's wealth and commercial energy, and shrewdly forged a relationship with the Church and citizenry that benefited all concerned. He also instigated work on the Tower of London.

Feudal England

During the early Middle Ages London's influence grew, while the kings of England were diverted by wars in France and Crusades to the Holy Land. Under Henry I London's citizens won the right to choose their own magistrates, and during the reign of the absentee king, Richard the Lionheart (1189–1199), the elective office of Lord Mayor was created.

England's medieval monarchs did not enjoy blind loyalty from London's citizens, whose strong trade and craft guilds, which still exist, created a self-determinism and power that often resulted in rebellions. The Palace of Westminster became the seat of government, and one of the reputed reasons for its riverside site was that a mob could not surround it.

The Tower of London

By 1340 London's population hit around 50,000, but in 1348 disaster struck. The Black Death swept across Eurasia, killing 75 million. Details of the horrors in London are scarce, and there are no accurate figures on the final death toll; however, it is estimated that almost half of London's population was hit.

London was still little bigger than it had been in Roman times, but this was about to change. The decision by Henry VIII to break relations with Rome gave birth to the Church of England and also added property in the form of seized monastery lands, such as Covent Garden (once a convent garden).

The Elizabethan Era

Between the death of Henry VIII in 1547 and the coronation of his daughter Elizabeth I in 1558, religious persecutions and political intrigues drained the kingdom's coffers and influence. But under the 45-year reign of Elizabeth, England rose to unforeseen heights, with London the epicentre of a mighty kingdom. The defeat of the Spanish Armada in 1588 signalled the dawn of empire, as the British Navy took to the seas in search of riches. The prosperity of Elizabeth's reign was marked by the blossoming of English literature, with Shakespeare the jewel in the crown of literati including Christopher Marlowe and Ben Jonson.

Portrait of Elizabeth I, National Portrait Gallery

Revolution and Restoration

Elizabeth's Stuart successors, however, are remembered principally for their failures. In 1605 James I narrowly escaped assassination in the abortive Gunpowder Plot –

Guy Fawkes was discovered in the cellars of the Houses of Parliament about to light the fuse that would have blown up the king at the opening of Parliament on 5 November. This act is still commemorated annually on 'Bonfire Night' *(see page 99)*.

James I's son, Charles I, was even less popular and, by attempting to dissolve Parliament, plunged the country into Civil War. In 1642 the Royalists ('Cavaliers'), supported by the aristocracy, went into battle against the Parliamentary forces. The 'Roundheads', named after their 'pudding-basin' hairstyle, were backed by the tradesmen and Puritans, and led by Oliver Cromwell. The Royalists were defeated at Naseby, Northamptonshire, in 1645. In 1648 Charles I was found guilty of treason and beheaded. Cromwell assumed power and abolished the monarchy, and for a short period Britain was a republic. In 1653 Cromwell declared himself Lord Protector, remaining so until his death in 1658. However, by 1660 the country was disenchanted with the dreary dictatorship of Puritan rule, and the monarchy was restored under Charles II.

Disasters and Recovery

The relaxation of the Puritan mores was not long enjoyed. In 1665 a terrible plague stalked London, killing an estimated 110,000 people. Death, disease and decay turned the city into a madhouse, in which piles of bodies were left in its streets, until taken away by cart to be buried.

In 1666 disaster struck again, in the form of the Great Fire. About 80 percent of the old City burnt down, and 100,000 people were made homeless. Incredibly, due to a speedy evacuation, the number of recorded deaths is in single figures. Sir Christopher Wren was appointed joint head of a commission to oversee the rebuilding of the city, and though his grand schemes were never fully realised, he made a huge contribution to the new London, including rebuilding St Paul's. The Monument *(see page 69)* is his memorial to the fire.

Stained glass portrait of Dr
Samuel Johnson, Fleet Street

The final great confrontation between king and parliament involved James II, brother of Charles I. A fervent Catholic, James attacked the Church of England and disregarded the laws of the land. However, the people of England had no stomach for cutting off another royal head, and in 1688 James fled the country. The so-called Glorious (peaceful) Revolution ushered in William of Orange and Mary II to the throne, establishing a stable constitutional monarchy. Under William and Mary, a royal retreat was established at Kensington Palace.

Georgian Greatness

In the 18th and early 19th centuries, London was the capital of a world power. In the coffeehouses of the City and West End great men of letters such as Alexander Pope and Samuel Johnson held forth. Handel was court composer to King George I, and Kew Gardens and the British Museum were opened to the public. But there was a dark side to London – slums grew up south of the river and in the East End, and crime was rife.

Overseas the Empire was burgeoning, until a tax dispute caused a rift between Britain and the American colonies. This escalated into a war over independence, and, to the astonishment of George III, the colonists won. By the end of the 18th century, Britain was threatened with Napoleonic invasion, but Nelson disposed of the French fleet at the Battle of Trafalgar in 1805. Some 10 years later, the Duke of Wellington put an end to Napoleon's ambitions at the Battle of Waterloo.

The Victorian Empire

The crowning of the 18-year-old Queen Victoria in 1837 gave the name to England's most expansive age. The Empire building that was started in Elizabeth I's day was taken to new heights in the 19th century. Ships filled with the bounty of the colonies not only brought goods with which to trade at the East End docks, they also drew in new languages, cultures and citizens who helped to shape this cosmopolitan city.

In 1851 Victorian progression was feted at the Great Exhibition, held in Hyde Park in Joseph Paxton's vast, specially designed iron-and-glass Crystal Palace. Transported south of the Thames to Sydenham in 1852, the edifice gave its name to a new Victorian suburb, Crystal Palace; sadly, the grandiose building itself burned down in 1936.

With the money taken at the Great Exhibition, Prince Albert, Queen Victoria's consort, realised his ambition: a centre of learning in the form of the Victoria and Albert Museum. This was followed by the Queen's tributes to her husband, the Royal Albert Hall and Royal Albert Memorial.

However, while the rich grew fatter, the poor were increasingly wretched, and the pen of Charles Dickens pricked many a middle-class conscience with his portrayal of the mis-

Blue Plaques

In 1867 a blue ceramic plaque was erected on the front of 24 Holles Street by the Royal Society of Arts (RA) to commemorate Lord Byron, who was born there. Across London there are now around 800 such plaques, each giving facts about the person concerned. The awarding of a plaque is haphazard – many are put up because descendants propose the suggestion to English Heritage; however, the person being remembered must have been dead for at least 20 years. The range has so far been dominated by politicians and artists.

Monet's *Thames Below Westminster Bridge*

ery and hopelessness of the souls condemned to poverty in this 'prosperous' city. London was growing rapidly, and by 1861 it had 3 million inhabitants. To house the newcomers pouring into the city looking for work, the East End slums expanded. The boundaries of London were pushed well out into the countryside with the development of public transport. Newly invented omnibuses, trains and, in 1863, the world's first underground railway created a new breed of London citizen: the commuter.

Two World Wars

In 1915 the German Zeppelins dropped the first bombs on London, and World War I left London's young generation grossly depleted. This was a mere foretaste of what was to come 25 years later – Hitler's Blitzkrieg rained bombs down on London between September 1940 and May 1941, during which the city experienced 57 consecutive nights of bombing. In June 1944 the rockets known as 'doodlebugs' were launched, battering London until March 1945. By the end of the war London's death toll was over 30,000, with 3.5 million homes damaged or destroyed. Through it all strode Winston Churchill, the indomitable spirit of wartime Britain.

Post-War Boom

Life in post-war Britain was spent clearing rubble and living frugally. By the 1950s, however, spirits were lifting, and, 100 years after the success of the Great Exhibition, the arts were feted again in the capital in 1951 at the Festival of Britain. The greatest legacy of the festival was the South Bank Centre, an arts complex built south of the Thames. London enjoyed a huge boom of popularity into the 1960s when a stream of rock and rollers, artists and fashion designers put London firmly on the map. Photographers, movie-makers and writers of the day chronicled the times, glamorising life in the British capital. The explosion of anarchic punk culture in the 1970s was followed by the rampant materialism of Thatcherism and Conservative rule from 1979 to 1997.

Labour's Legacy

Labour's landslide victory in the 1997 election (repeated in 2001), under Tony Blair, was welcomed by most Londoners. As areas of the city including Bankside were regenerated and London creatives dominated the arts, the British capital was celebrated in the press as 'the coolest place on the planet'. The millennium saw more successful developments, including the London Eye and Tate Modern.

Swinging London

Stars of the 1960s who brought glory to London include The Beatles, The Kinks and the Rolling Stones, models from Twiggy to Jean Shrimpton and hip fashion designers Mary Quant and Ossie Clark.

The Labour government decided to restore a measure of self-government to the capital by creating an elected mayor. Changes introduced by the first such mayor, Ken Livingstone, include a daily 'congestion charge' aimed at tackling the capital's traffic jams – a scheme that has so far managed to stall the rocketing traffic levels in Central London. The money raised must by law be spent on London transport.

Labour's popularity had slipped significantly by the 2005 election, thanks in no small part to Blair's controversial decision to take the country to war in Iraq. Despite this, the government was re-elected, although its majority was far smaller than in the elections of 1997 and 2001.

On 7 July 2005 London suffered a severe blow when, in Britain's first suicide-bombing, terrorists hit Underground and bus targets in the capital, killing 52 people and injuring around 700. The 'stoicism and resilience of the people of London' was praised by Blair, but the attacks still prompted a marked drop in tourism. Boosts such as the city's election as the host of the 2012 Olympics should help to restore confidence in this most cosmopolitan of cities.

City Hall – the Mayor of London's headquarters

Mayoral elections are due in May 2008 and Livingstone will face a spirited challenge from Conservative MP and television personality Boris Johnson. Meanwhile, urban renewal continues apace, with Kings Cross, home to the new Eurostar terminal at St Pancras Station, and Stratford, central to the 2012 Olympic Park, among the areas set for improvement.

Historical Landmarks

AD43 Emperor Claudius establishes the trade port of Londinium.

61 Boudicca sacks the city but is defeated, and London is rebuilt.

c.200 City wall built. London becomes the capital of Britannia Superior.

410 Romans withdraw to defend Rome. London falls into decline.

884 London becomes the capital under Alfred the Great.

1348–9 Black Death wipes out about 50 percent of London's population.

1534 Henry VIII declares himself head of the Church of England.

16th century London is the capital of Elizabeth I's mighty kingdom.

1605 Guy Fawkes attempts to blow up James I and parliament.

1642–9 Civil war between Cavalier Royalists and republican Roundheads.

1665 Plague hits London again, killing around 110,000 citizens.

1666 Great Fire of London.

1837–1901 Victorian Empire-building and the Industrial Revolution.

1851 Great Exhibition held in Joseph Paxton's Crystal Palace in Hyde Park.

1863 London Underground opens its first line, the Metropolitan line.

1888 The serial murderer known as Jack the Ripper strikes in Whitechapel.

1914–18 World War I. Zeppelins bomb London.

1922 British Broadcasting Company transmits its first radio programmes.

1939–45 World War II. London is heavily bombed.

1951 Festival of Britain. South Bank Centre built adjacent to Waterloo.

1960s London christened the capital of hip for fashion, music and the arts.

1980s Margaret Thatcher years. Several IRA bombs hit London.

1986 The Greater London Council is abolished by Thatcher.

1996 Shakespeare's Globe opens on Bankside.

2000 The Dome, London Eye, Tate Modern and Jubilee Line extension open to celebrate the millennium. Ken Livingstone elected Mayor.

2001 Greater London Authority is re-established under Livingstone.

2003 A 'congestion charge' is introduced to traffic in central London.

2005 London wins the bid for the 2012 Olympics. Terrorist bomb attacks on 7 July kill 52 and injure approximately 700 people.

2007 Gordon Brown succeeds Tony Blair as Prime Minister.

2008 London Mayoral Elections.

WHERE TO GO

There are as many opinions on the best way to tour London as there are places to see. Greater London is vast, sprawling for 610 square miles (1,580 sq km), so first-time visitors may find a ride on an open-top bus *(see page 115)* helpful in getting their bearings round the city centre. Once you've identified which area to explore, it's best to pound the streets, and seeing the city this way enables you to appreciate the variety of architectural detail that traces the city's development.

WESTMINSTER

The centre of official London, Westminster today is a far cry from its 11th century origins as a marshy island where Edward the Confessor built a church, 'West Minster', and a palace. Nowadays, it is home to Parliament, most of the nation's policy-making civil servants, and both the Prime Minister's and the Queen's London residences. London's *grand' place*, Trafalgar Square, is located here, complemented by two of the country's most important collections of art: the National Gallery and the National Portrait Gallery.

Trafalgar Square

Named after the naval battle that took place off Cape Trafalgar, southwest Spain, in 1805 at which Admiral Lord Nelson defeated Napoleon, **Trafalgar Square** is as good a place as any to start a tour of London. Long criticised as little more than a glorified, polluted roundabout, the square recently benefited from a lengthy construction project, spearheaded by Mayor Ken Livingstone. The north side is now completely

London landmark, Big Ben

pedestrianised and the square has become the focus for many of London's top cultural events and festivals.

Towering high above the square is the 170-ft (52-m) Nelson's Column. The statue of Britain's most famous maritime hero that tops the column recently underwent major cleaning and restoration. Adjacent are the stone lions by Sir Edwin Landseer that provide a popular spot for tourists after photo opportunities. Look out for the fourth plinth, in the northwest corner of the square, used to showcase temporary works of art by contemporary artists. Past commissions have gone to Mark Wallinger, Rachel Whiteread and Marc Quinn.

Sitting by the fountain in Trafalgar Square

National Gallery

Dominating the north side of the square is the **National Gallery** (<www.national gallery.org.uk>; open daily 10am–6pm, Wed until 9pm; free except some special exhibitions), which houses Britain's finest collection of European art from 1250 to 1900. The gallery was founded in 1824, when a private collection of 38 paintings was acquired by the British Government for £60,000 and exhibited in the owner's house at 100 Pall Mall. As the collection grew, a new building to accommodate it was planned. William Wilkins' grand neoclassical building opened in

1834 in the then-recently created Trafalgar Square.

Nelson on his column

The Sainsbury Wing, to the west of Wilkins' building, was added in 1991. Designed by the American architect Robert Venturi in witty postmodern style, it was famously denounced by the Prince of Wales as 'a monstrous carbuncle' (something of an overstatement); it is now a well-established addition to the National Gallery. The two buildings are bridged by a circular link, and the pleasant paved area between the two buildings offers a short-cut to Leicester Square *(see page 37)*.

The **collection**, which contains over 2,000 works, is divided into four sections: the Sainsbury Wing, the West Wing, the North Wing and the East Wing; within each section the paintings are arranged by school. The Sainsbury Wing houses paintings from 1250 to 1500, including Jan van Eyck's *Arnolfini Portrait* and Botticelli's *Venus and Mars*. The West Wing contains paintings from 1500 to 1600, including Leonardo da Vinci's *The Virgin of the Rocks*, Titian's *Bacchus and Ariadne* and Holbein the Younger's *The Ambassadors*. Paintings from 1600 to 1700 are exhibited in the North Wing, where you can admire Velázquez's *Rokeby Venus*, Rembrandt's *Self Portrait*, and Van Dyck's *Equestrian Portrait of Charles I*. The East Wing covers art from 1700 to 1900 and includes works by the English painters Constable and Gainsborough and Impressionists such as Monet, Van Gogh, Cézanne and Renoir.

National Portrait Gallery

The **National Portrait Gallery** (2 St Martin's Place; <www. npg.org.uk>; open daily 10am–6pm, Thur–Fri until 9pm; free except special exhibitions) was founded in 1856 as a 'Gallery of the Portraits of the most eminent persons in British History'. Additions to the collection have always been determined by the status of the sitter and historical importance of the portrait, not by their quality as works of art. Highlights include Holbein's drawing of Henry VII and his son Henry VIII, a life-like portrait of Queen Elizabeth I, in brocade and pearls, and self-portraits of Hogarth, Gainsborough and Reynolds. More recent subjects include Martin Amis, David Beckham and Tony Blair.

St-Martin-in-the-Fields

Located at the northeast corner of the square is the church of **St Martin-in-the-Fields** (tel: 020 7766 1100; <www.smitf. org>; open Mon–Wed 8am–8.30pm, Thur–Sat 8am–10.30pm, Sun noon–6.30pm; free), the oldest building in Trafalgar Square, built in 1724 by a Scottish architect, James Gibbs, when this venue was literally in fields outside the city. This is the parish church of the royal family and was so fashionable in the 18th century that pews were rented out on an annual basis. (The royal box is on the left of the altar.) Nell Gwynne, mistress of Charles II, is one of several famous people buried here. The crypts, which house a soup kitchen for the homeless, a café and brass-rubbing centre, were an air raid shelter in World War II. The church is renowned for its classical and jazz concerts, held at lunchtimes (usually free) and in the evenings.

St James's

On the southwest side of Trafalgar Square, Admiralty Arch frames a splendid view of the Mall, the sweeping boulevard that edges **St James's Park**. The park is the oldest of the

St James's Park

royal parks built by Charles II, who had been exiled in France and wanted to re-create the formal gardens he had admired there. The bird sanctuary on Duck Island is now home to exotic waterfowl and pelicans (the legacy of a pair presented to Charles II by the Russian ambassador in 1665).

St James's Palace (closed to the public), north of the Mall, was built as a hunting lodge in 1532 by Henry VIII and is now the London home and office of the Prince of Wales. The palace was the official residence of the court before Buckingham Palace was first used for that purpose in 1837.

St James's, the area north of the park that derives its name from the palace, is the epitome of aristocratic London and the heart of clubland in the old-fashioned sense (gentlemen's clubs not nightclubs). In its 18th-century heyday it was an upper-class male bastion; nowadays, there are fewer than 30 clubs, but the district is still home to centuries-old wine merchants, milliners, shirtmakers (notably on Jermyn Street) and shoemakers who cater for discerning masculine tastes. At the east end of elegant Pall Mall is the Duke of York's Column, a memorial to George III's impecunious son, who was the Commander-in-Chief of the British Forces. The Duke died with debts of over £2 million, and the statue was paid for by withholding one day's pay from every officer and soldier.

Also on the north side of the Mall, in Carlton Terrace, is one of London's most controversial public spaces for contemporary art, the **Institute of Contemporary Arts**, or **ICA** (box office tel: 020 7930 3647; <www.ica.org.uk>; galleries open daily noon–7.30pm, Thur until 9pm; admission charge). In addition to the gallery spaces, where changing exhibitions are held, the centre is home to an excellent café/restaurant, a bar (comedy and other events are sometimes staged here), a theatre, a bookshop and two cinema screens, where art-house movies are shown.

Buckingham Palace

Buckingham Palace

Crowning the west end of the Mall is **Buckingham Palace** ◄
(<www.royal.gov.uk>; open Aug–Sept daily 9.45am–6pm,
open Mar–Apr for private tours only; admission charge), the
Queen's main London residence. Built in 1702 for the Duke
of Buckingham, the palace was bought by George III, then
enlarged for George IV from 1825 by the architect John
Nash. The main façade is a later addition – by Aston Webb
in 1913. The Queen and Duke of Edinburgh occupy about
12 of the palace's 650 rooms, on the first floor of the north
wing. If the Queen is in residence, the royal standard flies
from the central flagpole.

The building was opened to the public in 1993 to help pay
for the repairs to the fire-ravaged Windsor Castle, and now
partly opens in summer/early autumn when the Queen is
away. Rooms open to the public include the Dining Room,
Music Room, White Drawing Room and Throne Room.

The Queen has one of the world's best private art collections, comprising about 9,000 works, including exceptional
drawings by Leonardo da Vinci and royal portraits by Holbein and Van Dyck. A selection is on show in the **Queen's
Gallery** (Buckingham Palace Road; <www.royal.gov.uk>;
open daily 10am–5.30pm; admission charge).

Most people in the crowds outside Buckingham Palace
come to see the Changing of the Guard at 11.30am (daily
May–July, alternate mornings Aug–Apr). The New Guard,
which marches up from Wellington Barracks, meets the Old
Guard in the forecourt of the palace, and they exchange sym-
bolic keys to the accompaniment of regimental music.

Whitehall

Whitehall is the area of government buildings that extends
from Trafalgar Square to Parliament Square. The name comes
from Henry VIII's Palace of Whitehall, of which the Ban-

'Number 10'

queting House *(see below)* is the only surviving part. The **Horse Guards**, on the west side of Whitehall, duly maintain their traditional sentry posts, as this is still the official entry to the royal palaces, even though Whitehall burned down in 1698, and St James's Palace has long ceased to be the main royal residence.

Opposite Horse Guards Parade is **Banqueting House** (<www.hrp.org.uk>; open Mon–Sat 10am–5pm; admission charge), built in 1619 by Inigo Jones for James I as England's first Renaissance building and inspired by Jones's hero, the 16th-century Italian master Palladio. Its major feature is a splendid ceiling by Rubens, commissioned by Charles I. Ironically, it was in front of this building that Charles was beheaded in 1649. Just a few yards away is **10 Downing Street** (<www.number10.gov.uk>), office and residence of the prime minister since 1735. Barriers at the end of Downing Street prevent public access to 'Number 10'.

Whitehall becomes Parliament Street at the junction with the **Cenotaph**, a memorial commemorating the dead of both world wars. Heading along Parliament Street you pass the imposing headquarters of the Treasury. At the end of King Charles Street and 10ft (3m) underground are the **Churchill Museum and Cabinet War Rooms** (King Charles Street; <http://cwr. iwm.org.uk>; open daily 9.30am–6pm; admission charge), where you can visit Churchill's World War II command post and a museum about his life and work.

The Houses of Parliament

The neo-Gothic Victorian triumph on the banks of the Thames is the **Palace of Westminster** (<www.parliament.uk>; open for tours Aug Mon–Tues and Fri–Sat 9.15am–4.30pm, Wed–Thur 1.15–4.30; Sept Mon and Fri–Sat 9.15am–4.30pm, Tues–Thur 1.15–4.30; admission charge), better known as the Houses of Parliament. At other times of year (Oct–July) UK residents can contact their MP to request a free tour or free tickets to watch a parliamentary debate (Prime Minister's Question Time is on Wednesdays from noon) and overseas residents can obtain tickets for debates by queueing on the day.

The original palace was built for Edward the Confessor, c.1065, and for 400 years it was a royal residence. The only remaining medieval part of the Palace is Westminster Hall, built in 1099. In 1834, someone disposed of several ancient wooden tally-rods in the basement furnace, and the resulting conflagration soon consumed almost all of the building. Many considered it a blessing to be able to rebuild the draughty old edifice. The architect Sir Charles Barry was the driving force behind the new design, a 'great and beautiful monument to Victorian artifice', which was completed in 1860.

Rodin's *Burghers of Calais* and the Palace of Westminster

The most famous element of Barry's design is the clock tower housing **Big Ben** (UK residents can arrange a tour by contacting their MP), a 13½-ton bell. The name is thought to commemorate Sir Benjamin Hall, Chief Commissioner of Works when the bell was cast in 1859; however, it may also have been named after a boxer of the day, Benjamin Caunt.

Westminster Abbey

Facing the Houses of Parliament is **Westminster Abbey** (20 Dean's Yard; <www.westminster-abbey.org>; open Mon–Fri 9.30am–3.45pm, Wed until 6pm, Sat 9.30am–1.45pm; admission charge). Much of the abbey was built in the 13th century in early English Gothic-style by Henry III; it remained an important monastery until 1534 when Henry VIII dissolved the monasteries after the Pope refused him a divorce. However, the abbey was still used as the royal church for coronations and burials, and all but two monarchs from William the Conqueror in 1066 were crowned here.

Beyond the nave, in the south transept, is **Poets' Corner**. Geoffrey Chaucer was the first poet to be buried here, in 1400. Behind the sanctuary are ornate **royal chapels and tombs**. The **Tomb of the Unknown Warrior**, west of the nave, holds the body of a soldier brought from France after World War I.

Just southwest of Westminster Abbey, on Victoria Street, is London's Roman Catholic cathedral, the outlandish Italian-Byzantine style **Westminster Cathedral** (<www.westminstercathedral.org.uk>; open Mon–Sat 7am–7pm; later on Sun; free), which dates from the 19th century. There are fine views from the top of its 330-ft (100-metre) striped tower.

Dead poets

Literary figures buried in Poets' Corner include Alfred Tennyson, Ben Jonson (who is buried standing upright), William Shakespeare, John Milton, John Keats and Oscar Wilde.

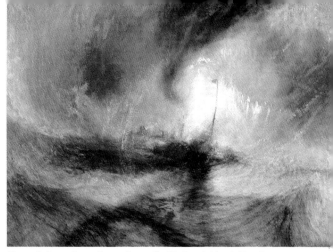

Turner's *Snow Storm: Steam-Boat off a Harbour's Mouth*, Tate Britain

Tate Britain

Slightly isolated, on the riverside near Vauxhall Bridge, is **Tate Britain** (Millbank; <www.tate.org.uk>; open 10am–5.50pm; free except some special exhibitions). It takes about 15 minutes to walk here from Parliament Square; slightly shorter is the walk from Pimlico tube station, from where the gallery is well signed.

Although somewhat eclipsed by its flash new sister gallery, Tate Modern *(see page 57)*, Tate Britain is still the main national gallery for British art, showcasing works from the 16th century to the present day. Some of the highlights of the collection include Hogarth portraits, Constable's *Flatford Mill*, Millais's *Ophelia*, the pre-Raphaelite paintings of Dante Gabriel Rossetti, Stanley Spencer's *The Resurrection, Cookham*, Francis Bacon's *Three studies for Figures at the Base of a Crucifixion* and David Hockney's *Mr and Mrs Clark and Percy*. Among the British 20th-century sculptors represented are Jacob Epstein, Barbara Hepworth and Henry Moore.

The Clore Gallery (an extension of the main building) was built to hold Tate's huge and magnificent J.M.W. Turner collection, which includes 282 oil paintings and over 20,000 other works by the Covent Garden-born artist.

If you're interested in visiting both Tate galleries, the Tate Boat runs every 40 minutes between Tate Britain and Tate Modern during gallery opening hours, and also stops at the London Eye. Tickets, available from both galleries, are valid for use all day for an unlimited number of trips.

The Selfridges shopfront on Oxford Street

THE WEST END

Despite its misleading name, which reflects the fact that it is west of 'The City', the West End is really London's shopping and entertainment hub. It's a sprawling part of town, stretching from Oxford Street in the north, through Soho, Chinatown and Covent Garden, to the Thames-side Embankment in the south. Though the area doesn't boast a lot of traditional 'sights', it is thronged with tourists and locals, day and night, as it is home to the greatest concentration of shops, theatres, clubs and many of the city's best restaurants.

Oxford Street

Bordered by Marble Arch to the west and the crossroads with Tottenham Court Road to the east, **Oxford Street** is the busiest and most famous – although admittedly not the most glamorous – of London's shopping streets. If you can brave the hoards of visitors (an estimated 9 million foreign tourists visit the street each year) and the impatient locals (around 60,000 Londoners work along Oxford Street), you'll

Busy West End traffic

find just rewards. From kitsch market stalls selling Union Jack T-shirts, to institutions such as **Selfridges** and high-street chains from Topshop to Gap, the shops here should meet all your retail needs.

Named after the Earl of Oxford, who owned land north of here from the 16th century, the road was built as a main route out of the city and was intended to link the counties of Hampshire and Suffolk. From the 1760s it began to develop as an entertainment centre. The Pantheon (replaced by Marks & Spencer in 1937) housed fetes and concerts, and Jack Broughton's amphitheatre, on the corner of Hanwell Street and Oxford Street, was famed for its boxing bouts and tiger baiting. By the late 19th century, however, the street was becoming established as a place for retail therapy. Furniture store Waring & Gillow opened in 1906, while the department stores, Debenham and Freebody (now Debenhams) and Selfridges – both of which have stayed loyal to the street – opened in 1909.

Marble Arch

 At the west end of Oxford Street is the monumental **Marble Arch**, erected in 1827 in front of Buckingham Palace and moved here in 1851 when it proved too narrow for the State coaches to pass through. The traffic island in which it now resides was the site of Tyburn Tree, a triangular gallows on which an estimated 50,000 people were publicly hanged between 1571 and 1759. Marble Arch marks the northeast corner of Hyde Park *(see page 76)*.

Regent Street

Perpendicular to Oxford Street is **Regent Street**, designed by John Nash as a ceremonial route linking Carlton House, the long-demolished Prince Regent's residence at Piccadilly, to the green expanse of Regent's Park further north. Despite the Regency connections, the elegant shop fronts disguise how young the street actually is – much of it was built in the 1920s, over 100 years after Nash began work. The road stretches nearly a mile (2km) from the stucco fronts and colonnades of the embassies around Langham Place, south across Oxford Circus (circus means traffic circle) towards the neon lights of Piccadilly and south again towards Pall Mall.

At the north end of the street is **All Souls Church**, completed by Nash in 1824. The tiny church is more akin to a Greek temple than an English church and was initially ridiculed by Londoners. Opposite this church is another London landmark, **Broadcasting House**, the home of BBC radio since 1932. Some of the most important transmissions in British history, including the 1936 abdication of Edward VIII and Prime Minister

Cheap tickets

Discount tickets for West End shows may be bought on the day of performance from the 'tkts' ticket booth (open Mon–Sat 10am–7pm, Sun 12–3pm) in the clock-tower on Leicester Square.

Neville Chamberlain's 1939 announcement that Britain was at war with Germany, have come from this building. The BBC still transmits 24-hour news, music and comment from here.

The main section of Regent Street – between Oxford Circus and Piccadilly Circus – is notable mostly for its massive shops, from Arts and Crafts flagship store, **Liberty**, to the seven-floored **Hamleys**, the largest toyshop in the world.

Patrolling Piccadilly Circus

Piccadilly Circus

Where Regent Street meets Piccadilly *(see page 44)* is **Piccadilly Circus**, whose illuminated signs first appeared in 1890. Three years later, a statue of **Eros**, Greek god of love, was erected as the Angel of Charity in honour of the philanthropic Seventh Earl of Shaftesbury; the Earl drove the broad thoroughfare that bears his name through the squalid slums that had grown up to the northeast. Nowadays, the statue serves as a handy meeting place for many Londoners. Other attractions here include the **Trocadero Centre**, a shopping-cum-entertainment arcade.

Leicester Square

East of Piccadilly Circus is **Leicester** (pronounced 'Lester') **Square**, a huge, rather unfriendly space dominated by large cinema complexes (most of the West End blockbuster premieres take place at the Odeon here), a big McDonald's and several brash nightclubs. Crowds often gather in the square to watch performance artists and musicians entertain, and if you want your portrait painted or are brave enough to have a caricature done, you'll be able to take your pick. Although at the moment the green area at the centre of the square is rather unimpressive, plans are afoot to improve the whole square and increase the amount of seating by 2010. **Leicester Place** links Leicester Square with Chinatown to the north. It is also home to the arthouse Prince Charles cinema *(see page 96)* and the French church Notre Dame de France.

Soho life

Soho and Chinatown

The area bordered by Regent Street, Oxford Street, Charing Cross Road and Shaftesbury Avenue, characterised by narrow streets peppered with independent bars, cafés and restaurants and some small shops and boutiques, has long been the focal point of London's bohemian nightlife. But life has not always been hectic in **Soho**. Before the 1666 Great Fire of London, this area was open land where people came to hunt – the name 'Soho' is thought to derive from a hunting cry. After the fire, the area's open land was used for new housing and, in the late 17th and 18th centuries, it was inhabited by noblemen and eminent society members. However, by the 19th century, wealthy Londoners were moving out to Mayfair *(see page 44)*, and Soho was taken over by the bohemian crowd. Its coffee houses and ale-houses soon became places for debate, founding a tradition that continues today in drinking clubs such as the Groucho Club.

Restaurants in Chinatown

In the 20th century the area became increasingly cosmopolitan. By the 'swinging sixties', Soho's seedier side came to the fore, and prostitution and the porn industry were rife. In 1972 the Soho Society was formed, and the group launched a campaign to clean up the area; by the early 1980s all sex shops had to be licensed.

London's x-rated cinemas and porn shops are still concentrated in Soho, but their presence no longer causes the outrage of former days. The area is now known primarliy as central London's main nightlife area and the focus of the gay scene. The streets are lined with bars that stay open till the small hours, jazz plays at venues such as Ronnie Scott's *(see page 95)*, and movers and shakers let off steam in dance clubs including Madame Jo Jo's. If you prefer more sedate pursuits, there's a concentration of theatres and cinemas in this area. There's also a great outdoor fruit-and-vegetable market in Berwick Street.

Adjacent to Soho, **Chinatown** is a tiny district that centres on Gerrard Street. Street names are subtitled in Chinese, and the tops of telephone boxes resemble mini pagodas. Eating out is the big attraction here.

Charing Cross Road

At the eastern edge of Soho is **Charing Cross Road**, London's street of bookshops – antiquarian and more mainstream. At the northern end of the street, in the shadow of the soaring Centre Point office block, the pavements are crowded with tourists heading for Oxford Street or lingering outside the grungy Astoria, one of the capital's main live-music venues (originally a Crosse & Blackwell pickle factory). If you're a budding rock star, make a detour down **Denmark Street**, where you'll find a huddle of music stores. Otherwise, take refuge in any one of the large yet restful bookshops, most of which have cafés, along the northern end of Charing Cross Road.

Covent Garden

With its pedestrianised cobbled streets, markets, variety of shops, opera house, theatres, cafés and bars, **Covent Garden** is one of central London's most appealing areas. It has a lively atmosphere and attracts a mix of people including opera- and theatregoers, street performers, shoppers and tourists.

All aboard!

In Covent Garden piazza the recently redesigned London Transport Museum (open Sat–Thur 10am–6pm, Fri 11am–9pm, admission charge; <www.ltmuseum.co.uk>) utilises many interactive exhibits to trace the development of the city's buses, trams and tube since 1800, as well as exploring the future of public transport in the capital.

The area covered by Covent Garden's main attractions – the market hall and its piazza – was once little more than pastureland belonging to the convent of Westminster Abbey. It was only after the dissolution of the monasteries that the land was given to the first Earl of Bedford. The Covent Garden that we know today took its form in the late 1620s, when the fourth Earl commis-

Covent Garden's market hall

sioned Inigo Jones to design buildings 'fit for habitation'. Influenced by his studies of Palladian architecture in Italy, Jones created the main Piazza, which consisted of St Paul's Church (now known locally as the actor's church, owing to its position in the heart of 'theatreland', as the Covent Garden area is often dubbed) and three sides of terraced houses. Although the design found little favour with Jones's contemporaries, it attracted rich, aristocratic families here.

Yet Covent Garden's popularity as a chic residential area was short-lived. In 1670, Charles II granted a licence for flowers and vegetables to be sold here, and in 1831 Charles Fowler's Market Hall was established as the market's permanent home. With the arrival of the market and the low life it attracted, the area began a slow decline and by the late 18th century it was best known for coffee shops, prostitutes and brothels. The market was held here until 1974, when it moved to its present site in Vauxhall, south London.

Royal Opera with the Floral Hall to the left

The Royal Opera

In the northeast corner of Covent Garden is the **Royal Opera House** (tel: 020 7304 4000; <www.royaloperahouse.org>), the third theatre to have stood on this site since 1732 (two previous buildings burnt down). The present one, which dates from 1946, was refurbished for the millennium at a cost of £120 million; facilities for the performers were improved, air-conditioning was introduced into the auditorium, and the glass **Floral Hall** (a delightful place for coffee) was rebuilt next to the main house. Both opera and ballet are performed here.

Strand and Embankment

Just south of Covent Garden, parallel to the Thames, is **Strand** (usually referred to as 'the Strand' by locals), a road that links Westminster to the City along a route opened in Edward the Confessor's time. It was along here that Eleanor of Castile's body was carried in 1293, with 12 crosses erected en route, one of which was Charing Cross. Today, the Strand is a street of shops and theatres, with the occasional architectural interest along the way such as the Art Deco Savoy Hotel and its glittering theatre. The short road in front of the Savoy is the only one in Britain where traffic drives on the right.

The church on an island at the eastern end of the Strand is **St Mary-le-Strand**. Built in 1724, it originally stood on the north side of the street, but, with the advent of the motorcar, the Strand was widened, and the church left in odd isolation.

Somerset House

Opposite St Mary-le-Strand is **Somerset House** (<www. somersethouse.org.uk>; courtyard and terrace open daily 7.30am–11pm, free; collections open daily 10am–6pm, admission charge), a grand example of neoclassicism, designed in the 18th century by Sir William Chambers. Located on the site of a 16th-century palace, Chambers' noble edifice was built to house government offices, including the Navy Board, and the three main learned societies of the United Kingdom: the Royal Academy of Arts, the Royal Society and the Society of Antiquaries. By the early 20th century the building was mainly used as the headquarters of the Inland Revenue and the Registry of Births, Marriages and Deaths. In the 1970s it was decided to return it to public use – it is now home to the **Embankment Galleries**, an exhibition space dedicated to presenting contemporary arts in innovative ways. The central courtyard is a fabulous space, housing an ice-rink in winter and hosting live music performances and an open-air cinema in summer.

Also in the complex is the **Courtauld Institute of Art Gallery** (open daily 10am–6pm; <www.courtauld.ac.uk>; admission charge, free Mon until 2pm), a compact and impressive collection of Old Masters and Impressionist and Post-Impressionist works.

Cleopatra's Needle

Parallel to the Strand is the riverside Embankment, which is the site of London's oldest outdoor monument, **Cleopatra's Needle**. Cut from the quarries of Aswan (c.1475BC), the 68-ft (21-m) Egyptian obelisk is one of a pair (the other is in New York) and was given to the British Empire by the Turkish Viceroy of Egypt in 1819. It took 59 years for the British to move it from where it lay in the sand to its present position – it was intended to stand in front of the Houses of Parliament but the ground there was too unstable. It is said that the sphinxes at the base are facing in the wrong direction.

MAYFAIR

Running west from neon-lit Piccadilly Circus *(see page 37)* and dividing two of the capital's most upmarket districts, Mayfair and St James's, is **Piccadilly** (once called Portugal Street). The road is one of the main routes in and out of the West End, and its name comes from the 'pickadills', or ruffs, worn by the dandies who frequented the area in the 1600s.

To the north of and including Piccadilly is **Mayfair**, one of the classiest areas in the capital and the most expensive place to land on the English Monopoly board. The second most expensive, Park Lane, bounds the area to the west, while Oxford Street marks Mayfair's northern side. The district takes its name from a riotous 17th-century fair and incorporates the bespoke suits of **Savile Row**, the commercial art galleries of **Cork Street**, auction houses Sotheby's and Bonhams, and **Old Bond Street** and **New Bond Street**, both of which are famous for their proliferation of designer flagship stores. In and among these elegant roads are dozens of narrow alleys and cut-throughs that give the visitor a flavour of London in the 17th century – it was at this time that the area was first transformed from a swampy plague pit where

Classy shopping on Bond Street

highwaymen preyed on passers-by to the fashionable place to be seen, and where Regency bucks such as Beau Brummell chaperoned respectable ladies on their morning strolls.

Royal Academy of Arts

On the north side of Piccadilly, west of Piccadilly Circus, is the 17th-century Burlington House, home of the **Royal Academy of Arts** (open Sun–Thur 10am–6pm, Fri 10am–10pm; <www.royalacademy.org.uk>; admission charge), or RA, entered through a huge arch and across a large courtyard and known for high-profile temporary exhibitions. Its less-known permanent collection includes Michelangelo's *Taddei Tondo*, Constable's *The Leaping Horse* and Gainsborough's *A Romantic Landscape*. Diploma work, submitted by Academicians on election to membership, includes Walter Sickert's *Santa Maria Maggiore*, Stanley Spencer's *A Farm Gate* and David Hockney's *Grand Canyon*.

Alongside the RA is the **Burlington Arcade**, built in 1815 and one of the oldest, most elegant of the capital's covered shopping promenades. This Regency promenade is patrolled by Beadles. In their top hats and livery, they ensure good behaviour, with 'no undue whistling, humming or hurrying'. Just opposite is **St James's Church** (197 Piccadilly; <www.st-james-piccadilly.org>) designed in 1684 by Sir Christopher Wren. It has a craft market and coffee house and holds regular classical concerts.

Fortnum's to the Ritz

At 181 Piccadilly is **Fortnum & Mason**, London's most glamorous grocers and purveyor of goods to the Queen for over 300 years. Enjoy the quintessential (if pricey) afternoon tea here or further along the road at **The Ritz** (150 Piccadilly; tel: 020 7493 8181, reservations essential; dress smartly). The Ritz backs on to **Green Park**, the smallest of the royal parks and the only one without flower beds – hence the name. The park was once a burial ground for lepers, and its lush grass is said to be a result of this.

At the western end of Piccadilly is **Hyde Park Corner** (*see page 76* for full information on Hyde Park). Just before the entrance to the park, facing Wellington (or Constitution)

Shepherd Market

The pedestrianised enclave off Mayfair's Curzon Street (or via Clarges Street or Half Moon Street from Piccadilly) was named after Edward Shepherd, who built the area in the mid-18th century. In the 17th century, the annual 15-day 'May Fair' was held here, hence the name of the whole area. Shepherd Market is the perfect place to relax, with bars and restaurants aplenty, many of which have pavement tables. Less salubrious, however, are the prostitutes who work the red-light district here.

Arch, is Apsley House, which has the highly enviable address of No. 1, London. Built by Robert Adam for the Duke of Wellington, it is now home to the **Wellington Museum** (149 Piccadilly; <www.english-heritage.org.uk>; open Tues–Sun, Apr–Oct 10am–5pm, Nov–Mar 10am–4pm; admission charge) and has a fine collection of Old Master paintings and memorabilia linked with the Duke.

Glitz at the Ritz

MARYLEBONE AND BLOOMSBURY

Despite their central location, both Marylebone (pronounced mar-luh-bun) and Bloomsbury are surprisingly genteel. Marylebone High Street and Marylebone Lane retain a village atmosphere, and many of London's top doctors have surgeries around Harley Street and Wimpole Street.

Cultural attractions in the area include the Art Nouveau **Wigmore Hall** (36 Wigmore Street; <www.wigmore-hall.org.uk>), a notable venue for chamber music, and the **Wallace Collection** (Hertford House, Manchester Square; <www.wallacecollection.org>; open daily 10am–5pm; free), a fine private collection of 17th- and 18th-century English and European paintings, porcelain and furniture, elegantly displayed in an 18th-century mansion.

East of Tottenham Court Road is Bloomsbury, London's literary heart and home to the British Museum, British Library and much of the University of London.

Inside the Sherlock Holmes Museum

Baker Street

Baker Street Underground station is the gateway to several local attractions including the **Sherlock Holmes Museum** (221b Baker Street; <www.sherlock-holmes.co.uk>; open daily 9.30am–6pm; admission charge). It pays tribute to Sir Arthur Conan Doyle's fictitious sleuth by creating an imaginative evocation of a Victorian apartment.

Madame Tussaud's

Nearby is one of London's most popular attractions, **Madame Tussaud's** (Marylebone Road; <www.madame-tussauds.co.uk>; open Mon–Fri 9.30am–5.30pm, Sat–Sun 9am–6pm; admission charge), where up to 7,000 people a day come to gaze at immobile effigies of various celebrities with glass-fibre bodies and wax heads. The museum was founded in 1835 by Marie Tussaud, who prepared death masks of famous victims of the guillotine during the French Revolution. Those gory beginnings are echoed in the Chamber of Horrors. The London Planetarium next door is no longer open to the public.

Regent's Park

Further along Baker Street is **Regent's Park**, an elegant 470-acre (190-ha) space surrounded by smart Regency terraces. Within the park are formal gardens, an open-air theatre, where Shakespeare's plays are staged in summer, and a boating lake. Regent's Canal runs through the north of the park.

Also located in the park is **London Zoo** (<www.zsl.org/zsl-london-zoo>; open Mar–Sept 10am–5.30pm, Oct–Feb 10am–4pm; admission charge), which is home to more than 8,000 animals, from lions and tigers to gorillas and hippos, and runs many breeding programmes for endangered species.

Northwest of the park is **Lord's Cricket Ground** (<www.lords.org>; tours Mon–Fri noon and 2pm, Sat–Sun 10am, noon and 2pm; admission charge), the ancestral home of cricket. To visit the ground, the portrait-lined Long Room through which players walk on their way to the field, and the memorabilia-packed MCC Museum, you have to take a 100-minute tour, which runs daily except on important match days.

The British Museum

The **British Museum** (Great Russell Street; <www.british-museum.org>; open Sat–Wed 10am–5.30pm, Thur–Fri 10am–8.30pm; free), opened in 1759, is the nation's greatest treasure house, with items from neolithic antiquities to 20th-century manuscripts. The main entrance is via the steel-and-glass-roofed Great Court, Europe's largest covered space, in the middle of

So much to see

The British Museum owns some 6½ million artefacts. To devote just 60 seconds to each one you'd have to tour the museum, without sleep or meal breaks, for more than 12 years.

which is the grand former main reading room, now an information centre. Behind the famous Athenian frontage are the 5th-century BC Elgin Marbles 'rescued' by Lord Elgin from the Parthenon in Athens in 1801, and the linguist's codebook, the Rosetta Stone, the key that unlocked the mysteries of ancient Egyptian hieroglyphics. There are excellent Assyrian, Egyptian and Roman artefacts in the main museum, including the world's richest collection of Egyptian mummies and funery art, the exquisite 1st-century Roman Portland Vase and the Nereid Monument, an elaborate Turkish tomb dating from 380BC.

Though a world museum, it is guardian of the great British treasures, too, including the Sutton Hoo trove from a burial ship of an Anglo-Saxon king, the 7th-century Lindisfarne Gospels and Lindow man, a Briton killed 2,000 years ago and preserved in a peat bog. The African Galleries display several 16th-century bronzes from Benin City.

The Great Court of the British Museum

Publishers' Bloomsbury

In the early 20th century Bloomsbury was home to Virginia Woolf, Vanessa Bell, Duncan Grant, Dora Carrington, Roger Fry and Queen Victoria's biographer, Lytton Strachey, known collectively as the 'Bloomsbury set'. Although their inclinations spread across painting, philosophy and writing, their connection was to challenge the conventions of the day. At that time publishing was a major industry in the area, with publishers including the Bloomsbury set's own Hogarth Press. Many imprints, however, have since moved to cheaper premises, but the bookishness of the area remains in the shops around Museum and Great Russell streets. Academia continues at the **University of London**, with the University's headquarters housed in the imposing Modernist tower of **Senate House** (1936).

King's Cross and St Pancras

The area around King's Cross and St Pancras stations, for many years run down and sleazy, is in the process of being regenerated into a new cultural zone. The first element to be completed is **St Pancras Station** itself. The immense Victorian Gothic red-brick and glass edifice has been renovated and extended, and is now London's Eurostar terminus.

The **British Library** used to be housed in the British Museum, but as the museum collection grew, it was decided to move the 9 million books, including a Gutenberg Bible, the Magna Carta and original texts by Shakespeare and Dickens, to new premises (96 Euston Road; <www.bl.uk>), near St Pancras. Galleries display some of the library's treasures, ranging from a 3rd-century biblical manuscript to original copies of Beatles' lyrics.

Nearby, the excellent new **Wellcome Collection** (183 Euston Road; <www.wellcomecollection.org>; open Tue–Sat 10am–6pm, Thur until 10pm, Sun 11am–6pm; free) showcases an eclectic mix of art and medical artefacts, including shrunken heads, a chastity belt and Napoleon Bonaparte's toothbrush.

THE SOUTH BANK

The area south of the Thames, from County Hall (opposite Westminster) to Southwark, further east, is an historic part of London. The first bridge across the Thames was built by the Romans near London Bridge, and the community around it developed as an alternative to the City, as it lay beyond the City's jurisdiction. In Shakespeare's day this was a place for showing unlicensed plays and setting up brothels, and it retained its reputation as an area of vice well into the 19th century.

In the late 20th century the area was transformed into a vibrant cultural centre; warehouses were renovated and converted into expensive flats, and the Underground's Jubilee Line extension transformed access here. Highlights now include the London Eye, South Bank Centre, Tate Modern and Shakespeare's Globe.

County Hall

Facing the Houses of Parliament is the neoclassical **County Hall** (<www.londoncountyhall.com>), built from 1909–22 and the seat of the Greater London Council, which ran London until an unsympathetic Thatcher government abolished it in 1986. It now houses two hotels, an aquarium, a games arcade and the Dalí gallery.

The **London Aquarium** (<www.londonaquarium.co.uk>; open daily 10am–6pm, last admission 5pm; admission charge) contains thousands of specimens representing 350 species of fish. Atmospheric sounds, smells and lighting have been used to great effect. It's worth catching the shark and rainforest talks (tel: 020 7967 8002 for schedule) and feeding times, when divers deliver a mix of mackerel and squid.

To the right of the Aquarium entrance as you face County Hall, **Namco Station** (<www.namcoexperience.com>;

The South Bank at night

open daily 10am–midnight) has video games, bumper cars and a bowling alley. The **Dalí Universe** (<www.daliuniverse. com>; open daily 10am–6.30pm, last entry 5.30pm; admission charge) offers a popular introduction to the Catalan artist, Salvador Dalí. It features 500 of his works (mostly reproductions), shown in themes. If you'd prefer to see some originals for free, head for Tate Modern instead.

The London Eye

Towering over County Hall is the **London Eye** (<www.london eye.com>; open daily Oct–May 10am–8pm, June and Sept 10am–9pm, July–Aug 10am–9.30pm), the world's largest observation wheel, built to mark the turn of the millennium. At 450ft (135m), it is the fourth-highest structure in London. The 32 enclosed capsules, each holding 25 people, take 30 minutes to make a full rotation – a speed slow enough to allow passengers to step in and out while the wheel keeps moving. On a clear day, you can see for 25 miles (40km). Book ahead to avoid the queues (tel: 0870 5000 600).

Around Waterloo

East along the river from the London Eye is Waterloo Bridge and the South Bank Centre. If you take a detour directly south from Waterloo Bridge, you'll reach the cylindrical **BFI London IMAX Cinema** (tel: 0870 787 2525; <www.bfi.org. uk>), run by the British Film Institute and decorated on the exterior with a massive mural by artist Howard Hodgkin. Large-format film is projected on to a screen 66ft high by 85ft wide (20m by 26m).

Waterloo Road leads to the **Old Vic** theatre (The Cut; tel: 0870 060 6628; <www.oldvictheatre.com>), founded in 1811. A music hall in its early days, it became the first home of the National Theatre and is now a repertory theatre with Kevin Spacey as artistic director. Further along The Cut, the **Young Vic** (66 The Cut; box office tel: 020 7922 2922; <www.youngvic.org>) mounts an adventurous programme, staging experimental plays and giving young directors a chance to develop their art. With low ticket prices, it aims to make theatre accessible to all.

Imperial War Museum

South of Waterloo is the Imperial War Museum (Lambeth Road; <www. iwm.org.uk>; open daily 10am–6pm; free), housed in the 1811 Bethlehem hospital for the insane. There is much civilian material from both world wars plus the latest in weaponry. An audio-visual display recreates a wartime air raid on a London street, and visitors can experience conditions in the trenches during World War I. The museum's Holocaust Exhibition is built around the testimonies of survivors, from the origins of anti-Semitism to its horrific conclusion.

The Southbank Centre

The **Southbank Centre** (<www.southbankcentre.co.uk>) is Europe's largest arts complex, housing concert halls, a gallery, cinema and theatre. Recent developments have greatly improved area around the centre, which is now packed with lively restaurants and bars.

The **Royal Festival Hall** (tel: 0871 663 2500; open daily 10am–11pm), the only permanent building designed for the 1951 Festival of Britain *(see page 19)*, is a major music venue. In 1967 the 2,900-seat hall gained two neighbours: the 917-seater Queen Elizabeth Hall, for chamber concerts, music theatre and opera, and the more intimate, 372-seat Purcell Room. Work completed in 2007 restored original 1950s design elements and improved the acoustics of the main auditorium.

New restaurants and cafés outside the Southbank Centre

On the upper level of the Southbank Centre complex is the **Hayward Gallery** (<www.southbankcentre.co.uk/visual-arts>). The gallery's programme of changing exhibitions focuses on single artists, historical themes and artistic movements, other cultures, and contemporary themes.

Next door is the **National Film Theatre** (tel: 020 7928 3232; <www.bfi.org.uk>), Britain's leading arthouse cinema since 1952. With four

screens, an interactive 'media-theque' and a stylish bar and café, it holds over 2,400 annual screenings and events, from silent movies (some with live piano accompaniment) to world cinema.

The final building in the complex is the **National Theatre** (box office tel: 020 7452 3000; <www.national theatre.org.uk>). Opened in 1976, it houses three separate theatres under one roof: the 1,200-seater Olivier, the 900-seater Lyttelton and the Cottesloe, an intimate space with galleries on three sides.

The 3-m (10-ft) high letters on Albert Moore's Oxo Tower

Around Gabriel's Wharf

East of the National Theatre, past an 18-storey tower housing London Weekend Television, is **Gabriel's Wharf**, a group of shops and restaurants backed by a striking set of *trompe l'œil* paintings. Set back from the river, the Art Deco **Oxo Tower** has pinprick windows outlining the words 'Oxo', a gimmick that the makers of the beef extract of the same name designed to get round a ban on riverfront advertising. The tower has a public viewing gallery and a chic restaurant *(see page 142)*.

Further east, just beyond Blackfriars Bridge, the riverside walk leads past the **Bankside Gallery** (open daily 11am–6pm) home of the Royal Watercolour Society and Royal Society of Painter-Printmakers.

Tate Modern

Easily identifiable by its tall brick chimney, **Tate Modern** (Bankside; <www.tate.org.uk>; open Sun–Thur 10am–6pm, Fri–Sat 10am–10pm; free) occupies the former Bankside Power Station and houses the Tate's international modern collection and part of its contemporary collection. The main entrance, to the west of the building, takes you into the ground floor through a broad sweep of glass doors and then down a massive concrete ramp. The impressive space rising six storeys before you is the Turbine Hall, the old boiler room now used to house massive sculptural works.

The permanent collection, including work by Picasso, Matisse, Mondrian, Duchamp, Dalí, Bacon, Pollock, Rothko and Warhol, plus sculpture by Giacometti, Hepworth and Epstein, is housed on the third and fifth levels (changing exhibitions are shown on level four). Works are organised into four artistic movements: 'Material Gestures' – post-war Abstraction, 'Poetry and Dream' – Surrealism, 'Idea and Object' – Minimalism, and 'States of Flux', which covers Cubism, Futurism and Vorticism. The displays move backwards and forwards in time, showing the predecessors and sometimes the opponents of each movement, as well as how they shaped and informed subsequent developments and contemporary art.

Checking out an unusual sculpture at the Tate Modern

The gallery has a restaurant with great views, on level seven, and a café on level two, adjacent to the excellent bookshop. To beat the crowds, visit on Friday or Saturday evening.

The Millennium Bridge

Providing a link across the Thames from Tate Modern to St
Paul's *(see page 66)*, as well as some spectacular views up
and down the river, is Norman Foster's **Millennium Bridge**.
Said to resemble a 'blade of light' when floodlit, this innovative suspension bridge – its cables are strung horizontally
rather than vertically – opened in 2000. The crowds who initially surged across it caused the bridge to sway, and it had
to be closed for nearly two years of engineering adjustments.
Pedestrians can now cross the bridge without a wobble.

Shakespeare's Globe

**The Globe Theatre, rebuilt just
as it was in Shakespeare's time**

Bankside and Southwark are
the South Bank's most historic areas. They grew up in
competition with the City
opposite, but by the 16th
century had become dens of
vice. Bankside was famous
for brothels, bear- and bull-
baiting pits, prize fights and
the first playhouses, including **Shakespeare's Globe**
(21 New Globe Walk; box
office tel: 020 7401 9919;
<www.shakespeares-globe.
org>). The replica of the
1599 building opened in
1996 and is worth a visit
even if you're not seeing a
play. Thanks to the efforts of
the actor Sam Wanamaker,
who sadly died before the
project was completed, the

Globe has been re-created using original construction methods. The open-air galleried theatre accommodates 1,500 people – 600 standing (and liable to get wet if it rains) and the rest seated. The season runs mid-Apr–mid-Oct. The adjacent **Shakespeare's Globe Exhibition** (tours and exhibition open mid-Oct–mid-Apr daily 10am–5pm; mid-Apr–mid-Oct Mon–Sat 9am–12.30pm and 1–5pm, Sun 9am–11.30pm and noon–5pm; admission charge) enhances visitors' knowledge of the Bard. Shakespeare's plays were not only shown at the Globe but also at the **Rose Theatre** (<www.rosetheatre.org.uk>), Bankside's first playhouse, built in 1587. Globe tours also visit the Rose during afternoons in summer.

Southwark

Back on the riverside walk, by Southwark Bridge, is the **Anchor Inn**. The present building (1770–5) is the sole survivor of the 22 busy inns that once lined Bankside. Just behind is **Vinopolis** (1 Bank End; <www.vinopolis.co.uk>; open Mon, Thur, Fri noon–10pm, Sat 11am–9pm, Sun noon–6pm; admission charge). Occupying an area of 2½ acres (1 ha) under the railway arches, this 'wine museum' offers a visual tour through exhibits of the world's major wine regions. Individual audio units give access to four hours of recorded commentary, and the tour includes tickets for five wine tastings.

Like most country bishops, the bishops of the powerful see of Winchester had a London base. A single gable wall remains of **Winchester Palace**, their former London residence. The bishops had their own laws, regulated local brothels and were the first authority in England to lock up miscreants. The prison they founded, in Clink Street, remained a lock-up until the 18th century, and the word 'clink' became a euphemism for jail. The **Clink Prison Museum** (1 Clink Street; <www.clink.co.uk>; open Mon–Fri 10am–6pm, Sat–Sun 10am–9pm) recalls the area's seedy past.

Clink Street leads to Pickfords Wharf, built in 1864 for storing hops, flour and seeds. At the end of the street, in the St Mary Overie Dock, is a full-size replica of Sir Francis Drake's 16th-century galleon, the **Golden Hinde** (Clink Street; <www.goldenhinde.org>; open daily 10am–6pm; admission charge). The ship, launched in 1973, is the only replica to have completed a circumnavigation of the globe and has thus clocked up more nautical miles than the original.

Southwark Cathedral and Borough

Southwest of London Bridge, hemmed in by the railway, is **Southwark Cathedral** (<www.dswark.org/cathedral>; open Mon–Fri 8am–6pm, Sat–Sun 9am–6pm; free). In the 12th century it was a priory church, and it has a Norman north door, early Gothic work and a number of medieval ornaments. Shakespeare was a parishioner here, and a memorial in the south aisle, paid for by public subscription in 1912, shows him reclining in front of a frieze of 16th-century Bankside; above it is a modern stained-glass window depicting characters from his plays. John Harvard, who gave his name to the American university, was baptised here, and is commemorated in the Harvard Chapel.

Borough Market (<www.boroughmarket.org.uk>), just by the cathedral, is a food market dating from the 13th century. On Fridays (noon–6pm) and Saturdays (9am–4pm) a gourmet market bustles with up to 70 stalls. It's not cheap, but the quality is high and you can often try before you buy. Apart from organic basics such as fruit and vegetables, a wide choice of more unusual food is offered, with stalls specialising in potted shrimps, game and Spanish ingredients. If looking at all that food makes you peckish, the charcoal-grilled chorizo ciabatta, cooked up by the Spanish stall, is delicious.

A two-minute diversion down Southwark Street, past the splendid Victorian **Hop Exchange** (now offices), is the small

Fish stall at Borough Market

Bramah Tea and Coffee Museum (Southwark Street; <www.teaandcoffeemuseum.co.uk>; open daily 10am–6pm), which gives a history of the long-established trade in London.

Across Borough High Street from the cathedral, the **Old Operating Theatre and Herb Garret** (9a St Thomas Street; <www.thegarret.org.uk>; open daily 10.30am–5pm; admission charge) is Britain's only surviving 19th-century operating theatre. The Herb Garret, once a store and curing place for herbs, now documents their use in 19th-century medicine.

The Pool of London

Between London Bridge and Tower Bridge is the Upper Pool of London, a former hive of waterborne trade. **Hay's Galleria**, with its shops, stalls and restaurants, marks the first of the Surrey Docks on the south bank. *HMS Belfast*, a World War II cruiser, is moored here as a museum (<http://hms-belfast.iwm.org.uk>; open daily Mar–Oct 10am–6pm, Nov–

Feb 10am–5pm, last admission 45 mins before closing; admission charge). To its east, the oval-shaped glass building is **City Hall** (open Mon–Fri 8am–8pm), home to the Greater London Authority, the body that governs London.

The entrance to the **London Dungeon** (28–34 Tooley Street; <www.thedungeons.com>; open daily, hours vary; admission charge) is usually marked by queues of visitors. This theme park of gore focuses on London's bloody history.

Tower Bridge

The elaborate Gothic-style bridge looming into sight as you walk east is **Tower Bridge**. In the 19th century, a time of great industrial expansion, there was a need to improve circulation over the river without hindering the access of ships into London's docks. The result was this triumph of Victorian engineering, built between 1886 and 1894, a bridge that

HMS Belfast, with Tower Bridge in the background

could be raised, made from a steel frame held together with 3 million rivets and clad with decorative stonework. The bridge was opened amid great celebration by the then-Prince and Princess of Wales, on 30 June 1894. The entrance to the **Tower Bridge Exhibition** (<www.towerbridge.org.uk>; open daily Apr–Sept 10am–6.30pm, Oct–Mar 9.30am–6pm; admission charge) is on the north bank of the Thames. The semi-guided tour takes visitors through the bridge's history, from the controversy that raged over the need to construct it, to its electrification in 1977. You also get the chance to see most of the inside of the bridge, including the basement, turrets and raised walkways.

> **Leap of faith**
>
> In 1954 a bus driver was awarded a medal for putting his foot on the accelerator when, to his horror, he saw the bridge yawn open before him. The bus leapt over a 3-ft (1-metre) gap.

Butlers Wharf and the Design Museum

The old warehouses located just east of Tower Bridge contain a gourmet's delight. The gourmet in question is Habitat founder Sir Terence Conran, who has opened up several restaurants in the biscuit-coloured **Butlers Wharf**. Originally completed in 1873, and once the largest warehouse complex on the Thames, Butlers Wharf closed in 1972. In 1985 a development team chaired by Conran began transforming the area's buildings into a stylish shopping, dining and residential area at a cost of £100 million.

Adjacent is the **Design Museum** (28 Shad Thames; <www.designmuseum.org>; open daily 10am–5.45pm; admission charge), which was set up by Conran when the Victoria and Albert Museum declined to make a temporary design show permanent. The museum contains a collection of influential design and design classics, mainly from the 20th century. It also holds excellent, themed, changing exhibitions.

Old and new side by side

THE CITY

For most of the capital's 2,000-year history, the area between St Paul's and the Tower, generally referred to as the 'Square Mile', was London. Still known as 'The City', it has its own local government, led by a Lord Mayor, and its own police force. The network of medieval alleys and back streets is still evident, but today's tall buildings hum with banks of computers processing international finance. Teeming with life on weekdays, the City is virtually deserted at weekends.

The Square Mile extends from the highly ornate Law Courts (located at the junction of the Strand and Fleet Street) on the west to the Tower of London to the east, and from the Barbican in the north to the Thames to the south. This was the area originally enclosed by the Roman Wall *(see page 12)*, but is now firmly held in place by commerce.

Legal London

Legal London starts at the edge of the City with the **Royal Courts of Justice** (better known as the Law Courts), in an elaborate late 19th-century building on the Strand. On the other side of busy Fleet Street, a few steps along, a tiny alleyway leads to the gas-lit sanctuary of the area known as the Temple, which houses two of the four Inns of Court – Inner Temple and Middle Temple (not open to the public). In former times these were the residences of barristers and barristers-in-training, and today's barristers-in-training must still be members of an Inn. The Temple takes its name from its 12th- and 13th-century function as the home of the crusading Knights Templar.

On Chancery Lane is Lincoln's Inn, the oldest of the four Inns of Court. On a large square adjacent is **Sir John Soane's Museum** (13 Lincoln's Inn Fields; <www.soane.org>; open Tues–Sat 10am–5pm and 6–9pm first Tues of month; free), the former home of a prominent late 18th-century London architect. The house is just as Soane left it, packed from floor to ceiling with priceless treasures, such as paintings by Hogarth (notably *The Rake's Progress* series), Turner and Canaletto.

Off Fleet Street, famous as the former centre of English newspaper production, is **Dr Samuel Johnson's House** (17

Cockney Rhyming Slang

The original definition of a cockney is someone born within the sound of Bow bells, the clarion of St Mary-le-Bow in Cheapside in the City. The cockney accent has no use of the aspirant 'h', the 't' in the middle of words such as 'butter', or the final 'g' in words ending 'ing'. Cockneys traditionally speak in a rhyming slang, which supposedly originated among barrow boys who didn't want their customers to understand what they said to each other. A 'whistle' is a suit, short for whistle and flute, and 'trouble and strife' means wife.

Gough Square; <www.drjohnsonshouse.org>; open Mon–Sat 11am–5pm, till 5.30pm May–Sept; admission charge). It was here that the first definitive English dictionary was compiled.

St Paul's Cathedral

St Paul's (<www.stpauls.co.uk>; open Mon–Sat 8.30am–4pm; admission charge), the first purpose-built Protestant cathedral, is Sir Christopher Wren's greatest work. A tablet above Wren's plain marble tomb in the crypt reads: *Lector, si monumentum requiris, circumspice* (Reader, if you wish to see his memorial, look around you). Although Westminster Abbey hosts more national occasions, Churchill lay in state here in 1965, and Prince Charles married Diana Spencer here in 1981.

Historians believe that the first church on this site was built in the 7th century, although it came into its own as Old St Paul's only in the 14th century; by the 16th century it was the tallest cathedral in England. Much of the building was destroyed in the Great Fire of 1666. Construction on the new St Paul's Cathedral began in 1675, when Wren was 43.

The architect was an old man of 78 when his son Christopher finally laid the highest stone of the lantern on the central cupola in 1710. In total, the cathedral cost £747,954 to build, and most of the money was raised through taxing coal arriving in the port of London. The building is massive and the Portland stone dome alone – exceeded in size only by St Peter's in Rome – weighs over 50,000 tons. Generations have giggled secret messages in St Paul's Whispering Gallery, over 100ft (30m) of perfect acoustics. You have to climb 260 steps to reach it, however, and a further 270 to enjoy the view from the highest of the dome's three galleries

In the cathedral's crypt, the largest vault of its kind in Europe, is a treasury containing ceremonial vessels, a burial chamber and a chapel dedicated to members of the Order of the British Empire (OBE). The highlights of this cavernous

St Paul's

undercroft include the tombs of the Duke of Wellington (whose casket was so huge that it had to be lowered into its resting place via a hole in the Cathedral floor) and of Admiral Lord Nelson, who was foresighted enough to take a coffin with him to the Battle of Trafalgar.

The Barbican

North of the City is the concrete **Barbican** (Silk Street; bookings tel: 020 7638 8891; <www.barbican.org.uk>), an arts and conference centre opened in 1982. The cultural offerings here include art galleries, theatres, a concert hall (the Barbican is the home of the London Symphony Orchestra), cinema, bars and restaurants. Visit at lunchtime for free foyer concerts.

Just outside the arts centre is the excellent **Museum of London** (150 London Wall; <www.museumoflondon.org. uk>; open Mon–Sat 10am–5.50pm, Sun noon–5.50pm; free), which charts every aspect of the capital's long history.

The Financial City

The heart of the business district of the City focuses on the **Bank of England** (nicknamed 'The Old Lady of Threadneedle Street'). Imposing windowless walls rise impregnably, with seven stories above ground and three below. This is where the nation's gold reserves are kept. Opposite the Bank of England is the Neo-classical **Mansion House**, residence of the Lord Mayor of London. Adjacent is Wren's **St Stephen Walbrook**, whose dome is said to have been a rehearsal for St Paul's.

Northwest of the Bank is the **Guildhall** (Basinghall Street; open May–Sept daily 9am–5pm, Oct–Apr Mon–Sat, last admission 4.30pm; free), the town hall of the City of London. This building dates from 1411 and withstood the Great Fire and the Blitz. Step inside (in office hours) to see the ancient Great Hall. Here the centuries-old functions and ceremonies continue: banquets of state, the annual swearing-in of the new Lord Mayor in November and meetings of the Court of Common Council.

The glittering Lloyd's building

East of the Bank of England, along the ancient thoroughfares of Cornhill and Leadenhall Street, is **Lloyd's of London**. Lloyd's originated in 1688 in Edward Lloyd's Coffee House, where ships' captains, owners and merchants gathered to do marine insurance deals. Lloyd's moved to Richard Rogers' space-age building in 1986. A huge atrium rises 200ft (60m) at the heart of this steel-and-glass structure which, like Rogers' Pompidou Centre, exposes its workings to view.

The Gherkin

North of Lloyd's, at 30 St Mary Axe, is another impressive edifice, a 40-storey tapering glass tower, designed by Lord Foster and known affectionately as 'The Gherkin'.

In the shadow of Lloyd's is the Victorian **Leadenhall Market**, once the wholesale market for poultry and game, and now a handsome commercial centre. It has been prettified, and its magnificent Victorian cream-and-maroon structure now houses sandwich bars, stylish restaurants and boutiques, which attract city workers at breakfast and lunchtime. London's other steel-and-glass Victorian constructions – the railway stations – were also given facelifts during the 1980s building boom. Nearby Liverpool Street was overhauled along with the adjacent Broadgate, adding an ice rink at Broadgate Square.

South of here, back towards the river, is Christopher Wren's 202-ft (66-m) high **Monument** (Monument Yard; closed for refurbishment until Dec 2008). The Roman Doric column was designed to commemorate the victims of the Great Fire, which destroyed 13,200 houses and 89 churches. Its height matches its distance from Pudding Lane, where the fire is believed to have started.

The Tower of London

On the north bank of the Thames is the **Tower of London** (Tower Hill; <www.hrp.org.uk>; open Mar–Oct Tues–Sat 9am–5.30pm, Sun–Mon 10am–5.30pm; Nov–Feb until 4.30pm; admission charge). Encircled by a moat (now dry), with 22 towers, the building was begun by William the Conqueror in 1078. Over the years its buildings have served

St Katharine's Dock

Just east of the Tower of London is St Katharine's Dock, which once housed over 1,000 cottages, the 12th-century church of St Katharine and a brewery. In 1828 these were all destroyed to make room for a new dock. Nowadays, it is an attractive yacht marina, home to a variety of pubs and restaurants.

as a fort, arsenal, palace and prison, and housed a treasury, public record office, observatory, royal mint and zoo.

At the centre of the complex is the White Tower, built by William I after his conquest of England in 1066. The Tower, which was designed by the Norman monk Gandulf, has walls 15ft (5m) thick and contains the fine Norman Chapel of St John on the first floor. Henry VIII added the domestic architecture of the Queen's House behind the Tower on the left, which is where the Tower's governor lives. The most recent buildings are the 19th-century Museum and Waterloo Barracks, to the right of the Tower, which contains the Jewel House where the Crown Jewels are a major attraction. At the centre of the display are a dozen crowns and a glittering array of swords, sceptres and orbs. The Imperial State Crown, made in 1937, has 2,868 diamonds and is topped with an 11th-century sapphire. A moving walkway speeds you past the treasures, so, rather disappointingly, you can't linger.

Look out for the Tower ravens; according to legend, if they ever leave, the Tower and England will fall. New ravens are bred and their wings are clipped to ensure they stay. Also look out for the Beefeaters, who guard the tower and act as guides.

KENSINGTON AND CHELSEA

The Royal Borough of Kensington and Chelsea is central London's most expensive residential area. It is home to upmarket shops such as Harrods and Harvey Nichols, designer row Sloane Street and also takes in the King's Road, an influential fashion stretch in the 1960s. The borough has a royal palace, a fine park and a clutch of world-renowned museums.

Knightsbridge

Knightsbridge – the name of both the road and the area, and the only word in the English language with six consonants in a row – is located just south of the central section of Hyde Park. It is one of the most expensive chunks of real estate in London. Dominating the road is **Harrods**, probably the world's most famous store. Opened by Henry Charles Harrod in 1849 as a small grocer's shop, the present terracotta palace (whose façade is lit by some 11,500 light bulbs at night) was built at the turn of the 20th century. Nowadays, the shop's staff claim to be able to source any item you want, and it even has a dress code, which security men on the door ensure is enforced. A big attraction in store are the vast Edwardian

11,500 bulbs illuminate Harrods

Food Halls, which are exquisitely decorated with around 1,900 Art Nouveau tiles.

In more recent years, Harrods has also become a place of pilgrimage. In the basement, owner Mohamed Al Fayed has created a shrine to his son Dodi and Diana, Princess of Wales – while many regard it as tacky, it attracts visitors daily who come to pay their respects.

Southwest of Harrods and its more fashionable neighbour, **Harvey Nichols**, is Beauchamp (pronounced 'Beecham') Place. The former village high street is now home to some pricey restaurants and designer shops. **Sloane Street**, the main shopping artery, has back-to-back designer labels and connects Knightsbridge with Chelsea.

South Kensington

Familiarly known as 'South Ken', this area is best known for its museums, a legacy of the Great Exhibition of 1851, in which Prince Albert raised money to purchase 87 acres (35 ha) of land in South Kensington and make this the 'museumland' of London. The Victoria and Albert Museum, a vast showcase for the decorative arts, is the biggest and best known, but the Natural History Museum is well worth a visit, especially for the extraordinary building in which it is housed; the Science Museum completes the trio. South Kensington has a large French population, which makes for a number of very good patisseries and some of the best French bookshops in London.

Victoria and Albert Museum (V&A)

The first director of the **Victoria and Albert Museum** (Cromwell Road; <www.vam.ac.uk>; open daily 10am–5.45pm, till 10pm Fri; free except for special exhibitions), Henry Cole, began assembling the museum's collection in the year after the 1851 Great Exhibition. However, Queen Victoria only laid the foundation stone of the current building in 1899, 38 years after Albert died. Its 1909 façade is by Aston Webb, who also designed the front of Buckingham Palace. Inside is the richest collection of decorative arts in the world. Plans issued at the entrance should be used to select an itinerary.

The collection includes extraordinary groupings of sculpture, pottery, china, engravings, illustrations, metalwork, paintings, textiles, period costumes and furniture. The Chinese, Japanese and Islamic rooms on the ground floor showcase some splendid exhibits,

Dale Chihuly's glass chandelier at the entrance to the V&A

and highlights of the sculpture and fashion collections include Canova's *Sleeping Nymph* and an evening dress by Vivienne Westwood. On the far side of the John Madejski Garden are the spectacular Arts and Crafts-designed Morris, Gamble and Poynter rooms, with their stained glass and Minton tiles. Originally designed as the museum's refreshment rooms, they were recently restored to their intended function as a delightful café.

Natural History Museum

On the other side of Exhibition Road is the neo-Gothic pile of the **Natural History Museum** (Cromwell Road; <www.

nhm.ac.uk>; open daily 10am–5.50pm; free), built from 1873–80 and a fine space with a grand central hall. The Life Galleries have exhibits on early man, Darwin's theory of evolution, human biology, birth and whales (including a life-size model of a blue whale), but the biggest draw is undoubtedly the Dinosaur Gallery – the museum's showpiece is an 85-ft (26-m) diplodocus skeleton. There's also a crowd-pleasing animated model of a Tyrannosaurus Rex, which roars and smells authentically unpleasant. Other highlights include the Creepie-Crawlies section, which usually proves popular with children; a simulated earthquake in a mock-up of a Japanese supermarket (New Earth Galleries); and an escalator that rises up through a rotating model of the globe, giving the sensation that you, and not the globe, are turning.

Dinosaurs are the big pull at the Natural History Museum

Science Museum

Adjacent is the **Science Museum** (Exhibition Road; <www.sciencemuseum.org.uk>; open daily 10am–6pm; free), which traces the history of inventions from the first steam train to the battered command module from the *Apollo 10* space mission. Seven floors of exhibition space cover computing, medicine, photography, chemistry and physics. There are imaginative exhibits on genes and the future of digital communications. The vast Wellcome Wing houses an IMAX cinema and some flight simulators, whilst the new Launchpad gallery with its host of hands-on exhibits, is great fun for kids.

Kensington Gardens and Hyde Park

Hyde Park and the adjacent Kensington Gardens cover one square mile (2.5 sq km) – the same area as the City of

Reconstruction of the 1969 lunar landing, Science Museum

London. Although they are a single open space, they are two distinct parks, divided by the Ring or West Carriage Drive.

Kensington Gardens were once the private gardens of **Kensington Palace** (<www.hrp.org.uk>; state rooms open daily Mar–Oct 10am–6pm, Nov–Feb 10am–5pm; admission charge). The palace has been a royal household ever since the asthmatic William of Orange fled damp, polluted Whitehall. A number of monarchs were born here, most recently Victoria, in 1819.

The lake at the centre of both parks is called the **Long Water** in Kensington Gardens and the **Serpentine** in Hyde Park. On the Kensington Gardens side, next to the lake, is a statue of J.M. Barrie's **Peter Pan**. According to tradition, at 9am every Christmas Day, hardy swimmers dive into the lake to compete for the Peter Pan Cup.

The **Serpentine Gallery** (<www.serpentinegallery.org>; open daily 10am–6pm; free), housed in a 1930s tea house, stages cutting-edge art shows. Past subjects include Man Ray, Henry Moore and Cindy Sherman.

Enjoying Hyde Park

South of the Gardens is the **Albert Memorial**, a gilded tribute to Queen Victoria's consort. Designed by Sir George Gilbert Scott, it depicts the Prince as a god or philosopher, holding the catalogue of the Great Exhibition. Opposite is another of Victoria's tokens to her husband, the **Royal Albert Hall** (Kensington Gore; <www.royalalberthall.com>; open Thur–Tues 10.30am–3.30pm for tours only; admission charge). There are up to six hour-long tours of the ornate concert hall each day.

To the north of the Gardens is the **Diana, Princess of Wales Memorial Playground**, commemorating the late Princess, who lived at Kensington Palace at the time of her death.

To the east is **Hyde Park**, which, the Domesday Book of 1086 records, was once inhabited by wild bulls and boars. It was first owned by the monks of Westminster Abbey, but after ecclesiastic property had been confiscated in the Reformation, Henry VIII turned it into a royal hunting ground. It was opened to the public in the 17th century and then sold off in chunks by Oliver Cromwell, the Lord Protector. The Serpentine, which attracts swimmers all year round, was created in the 1730s as a boating pond, and boats can still be hired from the north bank. Harriet Westbrook, the first wife of the poet Shelley, drowned herself in its waters in 1816.

Two years earlier it was the site of a spectacular re-enactment of Nelson's victory at the Battle of Trafalgar. Generally, the park is known for quieter pursuits – William III's Route du Roi (Rotten Row) is where the well-to-do canter their horses. On the south side of the Serpentine is a circular ring of flowing water dedicated to Diana, Princess of Wales and opened in 2004.

At the northeast corner, near Marble Arch, is **Speaker's Corner**, where anyone can pull up a soap box and sound off – a tradition going back to the days of the Tyburn gallows, when condemned men were allowed to have a last word.

Kensington

A few yards from the peace of these parks is busy **Kensington High Street**, dominated by chain stores. If you take a few steps off this main thoroughfare, however, you'll find elegant squares with gorgeous old houses. Situated just next

Portobello Road Market

Notting Hill is a gentrified residential area with some of the grandest Georgian townhouses in the capital. The area is also home to the annual Notting Hill Carnival (see page 99) and the Portobello Road Market. Built on the site of a pig farm named after an English victory over Spain at Porto Bello in the Gulf of Mexico in 1739, it has developed over the past 50 years into a major antiques market.

The road accommodates three markets. The antiques market, at the south end (Sat 6am–5pm), elides into a food market where the traditional fruit-and-vegetable stalls have been joined by traders selling fish, cheese and more exotic foodstuffs from around the world (Mon–Sat 9.30am–6pm, early closing Thur 1pm). Next, a flea market mixing genuine junk with cutting-edge fashion operates under the Westway flyover, at the north end, on Fridays, Saturdays and Sundays.

to the neo-Gothic church of St Mary Abbots is **Kensington Church Street**, famed for its antiques shops. At the west end of Kensington High Street is the wooded **Holland Park**, home to a blitzed Jacobean mansion, Holland House, with Japanese gardens and peacocks.

Chelsea

Chelsea has long been at the cutting edge of London fashion. Mary Quant started it with the first boutique (long-gone) on the **King's Road**, and from the World's End (430 King's Road) avant-garde designer Vivienne Westwood and Malcolm McLaren gave the world punk in the late 1970s. Chelsea in the 21st century is more subdued, and the King's Road tends nowadays towards chain stores; however, a walk along it is still good for people-watching. From **Sloane Square**, the up-market **Sloane Street** connects Chelsea with Knightsbridge.

Founder's Day at Chelsea Royal Hospital

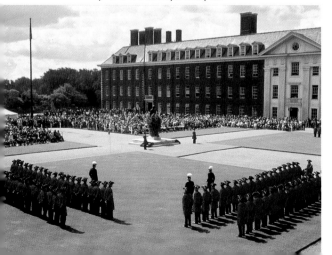

The Duke of York's HQ on King's Road became the new home of the **Saatchi Gallery** (<www.saatchi-gallery.co.uk>; free) in spring 2008. The gallery showcases the work of contemporary artists assembled by former advertising mogul Charles Saatchi. Previously based in County Hall, the gallery is best known for exhibiting Tracey Emin's *My Bed* and Damien Hirst's shark in formaldehyde.

The **Royal Hospital** on Chelsea Bridge Road, has been a Chelsea landmark since 1692. It is home to the Chelsea Pensioners, known for their scarlet coats, which date to the 18th century. Between here and the Embankment are Ranelagh Gardens, which host the Chelsea Flower Show every spring.

Continue down to the River Thames along Royal Hospital Road and turn into Tite Street. This attractive residential area is the epitome of bourgeois respectability but in the early 19th century it was very bohemian. Look out for the blue plaques on the street dedicated to Oscar Wilde (No 34) and John Singer Sargent (No 31). Turn right on to the Embankment and ahead is **Cheyne Walk**. The splendid houses here were on the water's edge until the reclamation of the Embankment in the 19th century. Blue plaques mark the former homes of pre-Raphaelite painter Dante Gabriel Rosetti as well as the author George Eliot. Just off Cheyne Walk is **Carlyle's House** (24 Cheyne Row; <www.nationaltrust.org.uk>; open mid-Mar–Oct Wed–Fri 2–5pm, Sat–Sun 11am–5pm; admission charge), home of the writer, Thomas Carlyle, until his death in 1881.

Another famous Chelsea resident was Sir Thomas More, who lived in Beaufort Street. In 1535 he was taken by boat to his trial at Westminster and later beheaded for refusing to accept the 'Oath of Supremacy', by which Henry VIII claimed to be equal to God. Sir Thomas intended All Saints Church (off Cheyne Walk) to be his last resting place, but his tomb actually contains his wife, Alice, as his head was taken to Canterbury.

NORTH LONDON

Easily accessible by Underground, North London has many attractions, including upmarket Hampstead, notable for its heath and literary connections, neighbouring Highgate with its cemetery, and elegant Islington, the stomping ground of the chattering classes. Camden is worth a visit for its busy, bohemian market and its pleasant canal area.

Islington

This borough, widely regarded as the territory of well-heeled socialists, symbolises the gentrification of London's Georgian and Victorian dwellings. Classic terraces can be found in areas such as Canonbury Square, where authors George Orwell and Evelyn Waugh once lived. The square is home to the **Estorick Collection** (39a Canonbury Square; <www.estorickcollection.com>; admission charge; open Wed–Sat 11am–6pm, Sun 12–5pm), a showcase for modern Italian art.

The crossroads at the heart of Islington's shopping district is called the Angel, named after a long-gone coaching inn. Adjacent is **Camden Passage**, an upmarket antiques arcade; more affordable bargains can be had at the street market held here on Wednesday and Saturday. At the south end of Islington is **Sadler's Wells** (Rosebery Avenue; tel: 020 7863 8198; <www.sadlerswells.com>), London's top modern dance venue.

Camden

Markets are also the main attraction in Camden. Cheap clothes aimed at the young are sold at Camden High Street (Thur–Sun 10am–5.30pm), while crafts are on offer at Camden Lock Market, off Chalk Farm Road (outdoor stalls Sat–Sun 10am–6pm, indoor stalls daily except Mon). Camden Lock is on the Regent's Canal, an 8½-mile (14-km) stretch of water running from Paddington to Limehouse in Docklands.

Regent's Canal at Camden Lock

Hampstead and Highgate

Exclusive **Hampstead** has long been a desirable address, especially among the successful literary set, and it still has its fair share of wealthy celebrity residents. Open spaces predominate. The 3-square-mile (8-sq-km) **Heath** is the main 'green lung', with Parliament Hill on its south side giving splendid views across London, as does the 112-acre (45-ha) **Primrose Hill** overlooking Regent's Park to the south. These are all welcome areas of parkland over which locals stride, walk dogs, fly kites, skate and swim in the segregated ponds.

The elegant **Kenwood House** (Hampstead Lane; <www.english-heritage.org.uk>; open Apr–Oct 11am–5pm, Nov–Mar 11am–4pm; free), which overlooks Hampstead Heath, showcases the Iveagh Bequest. The collection includes works by Rembrandt, Reynolds, Turner and Gainsborough.

Sigmund Freud, fleeing the Nazis in 1938, moved from Vienna to Hampstead. The **Freud Museum** (20 Maresfield

The poet John Keats (1795–1821) wrote much of his work, including *Ode to a Nightingale*, in the two years he lived in Hampstead. The building, Keats House (Wentworth Place; open May–Oct Tues–Sun 1–5pm) now houses memorabilia including his letters and a lock of hair.

Gardens; <www.freud.org. uk>; open Wed–Sun noon–5pm; admission charge) preserves his house as he left it.

A pretty hill-top suburb, **Highgate** is home to the grandest burial ground in London, **Highgate Cemetery** (Swain's Lane; <www. highgate-cemetery.org>; open Mon–Fri 10am–5pm, Sat–Sun 11am–5pm, Nov–Mar until 4pm; admission charge). Graves include those of Christina Rossetti, George Eliot and Karl Marx.

EAST LONDON

This part of London was the first stop for many of the successive waves of immigrants, whose labour helped to fuel the Industrial Revolution and build the docks through which much of the British Empire's trade passed. Poverty and overcrowding were endemic. Although many areas remain poor, a growing number have now been gentrified.

Hoxton, Spitalfields and Whitechapel

One such gentrified area is **Hoxton**, near Old Street. The transformation began when artists moved in, many creating studios in redundant warehouses. Art dealers and designers followed, and urban desolation became urban chic. Around Hoxton Square are a rash of hip bars and galleries.

The main attraction in the area is **Spitalfields Market**, a former fruit-and-vegetable market, which now has a variety of antiques and crafts stalls in the week and a buzzy bohemian craft, clothing and organic food market on Sundays. Near here is a museum with a difference, the wonderfully atmospheric **Dennis Severs' House** (18 Folgate Street; tel: 020 7247 4013; <www.dennissevershouse.co.uk>; open Mon evenings (by candlelight); 1st and 3rd Sun of the month noon–4pm, following Mon noon–2pm; admission charge, booking necessary). An American artist, Severs renovated this former 18th-century silk-weaver's house in the 1970s, creating a time capsule that assaults the senses – it looks, smells and sounds as if 18th-century Huguenots still live there.

Southwest, in Middlesex Street, **Petticoat Lane** market is busy with stalls on Sundays, although most just sell cheap clothes. Southeast of Spitalfields is **Brick Lane**, known for its proliferation of Indian restaurants. There are trendy bars and boutiques on the northern stretch. Responding to the East End's spiritual and economic poverty, a local vicar and his wife founded the **Whitechapel Art Gallery** (Whitechapel High

Brick Lane

Office workers in Docklands

Street; <www.whitechapel.org>; open Wed–Sun 11am–6pm, Thur until 9pm; free) in 1897. The gallery mounts high-profile changing shows in a lovely airy space.

Docklands

London's docks, made derelict by heavy World War II bombing and rendered obsolete by the new container ports to the east, were transformed in the 1990s. Their proximity to the financial institutions of the City made them an attractive location for high-tech office buildings, and the 850-ft tall (260-m) **Canary Wharf** complex was the first of several skyscrapers to spring up. The area is now a lively but somewhat sterile patchwork of glass, steel and concrete. The **Museum in Docklands** (No. 1 Warehouse, West India Quay; <www.museumindocklands.org.uk>; open daily 10am–6pm; admission charge) recounts 2,000 years of local history. Highlights include a 20-ft (6-metre) model of Old London Bridge and an evocative exhibition about London's role in the slave trade.

SOUTHEAST LONDON

North Londoners have long felt superior to those south of the Thames, and a North–South divide still exists, albeit largely tongue-in-cheek. The lack of an Underground network doesn't help Southeast London's immediate appeal. However, those willing to negotiate the network of overland trains will find riches from historic naval Greenwich to artistic Dulwich.

Greenwich

Long the favoured destination of nautical and science buffs, Greenwich enjoyed notoriety in 2000 as the site of the Millennium Dome. The great white tent was built to house a one-year exhibition for the millennium, but was a financial and critical failure. The structure has now been relaunched as 'The O2' and is used as an arena for concerts and sporting events.

There are plenty of other reasons to visit villagey Greenwich. The district can be covered in half a day and is at its busiest at weekends, when its craft markets are held. One of the nicest ways to arrive is by boat from Westminster or Tower Bridge, although you can also travel by Docklands Light Railway (DLR) from Bank or by train from London Bridge.

In dry dock on the waterfront is the **Cutty Sark** (Greenwich Church Street; <www.cuttysark.org.uk>), a sailing ship from the great days of the tea-clippers that used to race to be the first to bring the new season's tea from China. The ship is currently closed to the public after it was damaged by a serious fire. Luckily, at the time of the blaze many of the ship's timbers and its striking figurehead had already been removed to allow restoration work to take place. Repairs have begun and it is hoped that the ship will eventually reopen to the public.

Much of the land in the area is taken up by lovely **Greenwich Park**, at the top of which is Sir Christopher Wren's **Royal Observatory** (Greenwich Park; <www.nmm.ac.uk>; open daily 10am–5pm; free), where Greenwich Mean Time was established in 1884. It's a steep climb to the Observatory, but the views are splendid. A brass rule on the ground marks the line between the Eastern and Western hemispheres, making it possible to have a foot in both.

At the base of the park is the imposing **National Maritime Museum** (Romney Road; <www.nmm.ac.uk>; open daily 10am–5pm; free), which has been redeveloped to create 16 new galleries around a spectacular courtyard that is spanned by the largest glazed roof in Europe. It traces the history both of the Royal Navy and the Merchant Navy, as well as the colonisers and discoverers.

Opposite is the **Old Royal Naval College** (King William Walk; <www.oldroyalnavalcollege.org>; open daily 10am–5pm; free), designed by Wren, Hawksmoor and Vanbrugh, with gardens by André Le Nôtre. It was built as a hospital for naval pensioners to match Wren's Royal Hospital in Chelsea and was designed in two halves to leave the view free to the river from Inigo Jones' **Queen's House** (Romney Road; <www.nmm.ac.uk>; open daily 10am–5pm; free), a gift to Anne of Denmark from her husband, James.

The view from Greenwich Park towards Canary Wharf

The heart of Greenwich lies to the west of the park, where an attractive, old-fashioned **covered market** and neighbouring Greenwich Church Street are lively at weekends.

Dulwich

With leafy streets, elegant houses and a spacious park, Dulwich is an oasis of calm. It is largely the creation of one man, Edward Alleyn, an actor-manager who bought land in the area in 1605 and founded an estate to administer a chapel, almshouses and a school for the poor.

Dulwich College, which schooled the writers P.G. Wodehouse and Raymond Chandler, spawned the **Dulwich Picture Gallery** (Gallery Road; <www.dulwichpicturegallery. org.uk>; open Tues–Fri 10am–5pm, Sat–Sun 11am–5pm; admission charge) by combining Alleyn's collection with a bequest of paintings originally intended for a Polish National Gallery but diverted when the King of Poland was forced to abdicate. The building opened in 1814 as the country's first major public art gallery, with works by masters including Rembrandt, Rubens, Gainsborough and Murillo.

The Horniman

Just east of Dulwich, in Forest Hill, is the Horniman Museum (100 London Road; <www.horniman. ac.uk>; open daily 10.30am–5.30pm; free). Founded in 1901 by tea merchant, Frederick Horniman, the museum houses rich collections of ethnography and natural history.

SOUTHWEST LONDON

This wealthy area incorporates Wimbledon, synonymous with tennis; genteel Richmond, home to a pleasant shopping centre and a vast area of parkland; Kew, site of the UNESCO-protected Kew Gardens; and Hampton Court, where the 16th-century riverside palace was the favourite residence of Henry VIII.

Ham House

Reached along the tow-path at Richmond is Ham House (<www.national trust.org.uk>; open Apr–Oct Sat–Wed 1–5pm; admission charge), a furnished 1610 Palladian building set in lovely gardens.

Wimbledon, Richmond and Kew

This suburb hosts Britain's top tennis tournament in June/ July *(see page 97)*, and its history is captured in the **Lawn Tennis Museum** (Church Road, Wimbledon; <www.wimbledon.org>; open daily 10.30am–5pm; admission charge). The area is also known for **Wimbledon Common**, a large partly wooded expanse with nature trails.

The main attraction in Richmond is **Richmond Park**, grazed by herds of red and fallow deer and, at 2,350 acres (950 ha), the largest of the royal parks. The original royal residence in the park is the Palladian White Lodge (1727), now used by the Royal Ballet School. **Richmond Green** is the handsome town centre, lined with some fine 17th- and 18th-century buildings, and the remains of the 12th-century royal palace.

The nearby suburb of **Kew** is synonymous with the **Royal Botanic Gardens** (<www.kew.org.uk>; open Apr–Aug Mon–Fri 9.30am–6.30pm, Sat–Sun 9.30am–7.30pm; Sept–Oct daily 9.30am–6pm; Nov–mid-Feb daily 9.30am–4.15pm; mid-Feb–Mar daily 9.30am–5.30pm; admission charge). The 300-acre (120-ha) gardens were established in 1759 with the help of Joseph Banks, the botanist who named Botany Bay on Captain James Cook's first voyage to Australia. Other explorers and amateur enthusiasts added their specimens over the centuries, making this a formidable repository and research centre.

The gardens are beautiful, with grand glasshouses including the Palm House and Waterlily House, an orangery, mock Chinese pagoda and the 17th-century Dutch House, a former royal palace (currently undergoing major restoration). George III was locked up here when it was thought that he had gone mad. His wife Charlotte had a summerhouse built in the grounds as a picnic spot. Two small art galleries focus on horticulture.

Hampton Court

Located 14 miles (23km) west of central London and easily accessible by train from Waterloo or by riverboat from Westminster or Richmond, the Tudor **Hampton Court Palace** (<www.hrp.org.uk>; open Nov–Mar Mon–Sun 10am–4.30pm, Apr–Oct 10am–6pm; admission charge) was built in 1514 for Cardinal Wolsey but appropriated by Henry VIII in 1525, following Wolsey's fall from grace. Surrounded by 60 acres (24 ha) of immaculate riverside gardens and with a world-renowned maze, it was Henry's favourite palace – he spent five of his six honeymoons here.

At Kew Gardens

Although the State Apartments are sumptuous, featuring works by such gifted craftsmen as Antonio Verrio and William Kent, the highlights of the visit are the Great Hall and Chapel Royal. Also popular is the palace maze, which has been baffling royalty and visitors for some 300 years.

WHAT TO DO

L ondon has some of the greatest theatres in the world and is at the cutting edge of fashion, music and the arts. This chapter is an introduction to the multitude of shopping and entertainment opportunities available. For up-to-the-minute entertainment listings consult the weekly events' magazine *Time Out*; *Metro*, a free newspaper read by many Londoners on the tube; and *The Guide*, free with Saturday's *Guardian*.

SHOPPING

With over 30,000 shops, London is a consumerist heaven, and it's no surprise that people flock here from all over the world just to spend, spend, spend. However specialised your retail needs, you can be sure that somewhere in this sprawling city there's a shop that can meet them. And, unlike in many other European capitals, Sundays and summer holidays are not sacred. London is a year-round shoppers' destination.

While the size of the city makes it impossible to cover it in a week, from a shopper's point of view, London is relatively easy to navigate. The city is loosely divided into shopping districts, each offering its own experience; in some cases there are whole streets devoted to one theme. The underground is usually the quickest means of getting from area to area, while the bus system is excellent but less easy to navigate. Distances between some streets, such as Oxford Street, Tottenham Court Road, Regent Street and Bond Street, are short enough to walk.

For those wanting the best of European and international designer fashions, Knightsbridge, home to the high-class department stores Harrods and Harvey Nichols, has the high-

The Theatre Royal on Haymarket

est concentration of such shops. Haute couture names from Armani to Yves Saint Laurent sit next to established British designers. Old Bond Street and New Bond Street, in Mayfair, also offer a vast choice of designer labels. Savile Row, again in Mayfair, specialises in bespoke tailoring, and Cork Street, with its numerous galleries, is an art-lover's dream.

In the Piccadilly area, you'll find the upmarket grocer's Fortnum & Mason, as well as some of London's oldest shops, many of which hold royal warrants to supply the Queen and her family with goods. Nearby Jermyn Street specialises in shirts. Regent Street, with its impressive neoclassical architecture, is home to Britain's largest toy shop, Hamleys, and London institution Liberty.

Department stores such as Selfridges and John Lewis, and flagship stores of chains such as Topshop and Primark characterise Oxford Street, the capital's main shopping thoroughfare. Nearby Tottenham Court Road is dominated by electronics shops, selling everything from cameras to the latest in computer software, and interiors shops including Habitat and Heal's.

Although Soho has never quite lost its seedy image, between the sex shops are some great fashion boutiques selling hip urbanwear. Bookworms should head to Charing Cross Road, renowned for its second-hand and antiquarian bookshops. Covent Garden is one of London's more laid-back areas, with shops ranging from high-street and cutting-edge fashion boutiques to quirky specialists selling everything from teapots to kites.

Although the King's Road is no longer the destination for leading fashions, shoppers still flock to it for its popular chain stores and small boutiques. Kensington Church Street is a favourite destination for antiques lovers, with more than 80 dealers lining the street. Notting Hill, home of Portobello market, also has many fashionable boutiques.

London's numerous other markets include Spitalfields, near Liverpool Street. On Sundays this historic covered market is a great place to spot up-and-coming talent, as fashion and accessory designers run many of the stalls. The market has an organic food section too. Also on Sunday, nearby cobbled Columbia Road is busy with stalls selling every type of cut flower and houseplant imaginable and Petticoat Lane market does great cheap clothing.

Whatever your retail tactics, and whether you're spending out of necessity or just as a treat, London's shops won't disappoint.

Bond Street is home to many stylish boutiques

ENTERTAINMENT

Whether you're after theatre, opera, clubs or pubs, there is no shortage of entertainment in London.

Theatre

London's theatrical history goes back to a playhouse opened at Shoreditch in 1576 by James Burbage, son of a carpenter and travelling player. Nowadays, London's theatres, staging comedies, musicals and dramas, are concentrated in the **West End**. For same-day half price tickets for West End shows, visit the Leicester Square 'tkts' booth *(see page 37)*.

The Last Night of the Proms in the Royal Albert Hall

Other theatres include the **National Theatre** at the South-bank Centre *(see page 55)*, which stages innovative productions of the classics, some excellent modern pieces and the occasional rousing musical revival. The **Old Vic** *(see page 54)* specialises in revivals of the classics, while the nearby **Young Vic** *(see page 54)* leans towards more recent, experimental theatre. Chelsea's **Royal Court Theatre** (Sloane Square; tel: 020 7565 5000; <www.royalcourttheatre.com>) is famous for cutting-edge drama, and the buzzy café downstairs is a lovely place for a bite to eat or a drink whether you're watching a show or not. **Shakespeare's Globe** *(see page 58)*, on Bankside, stages works by the Bard and his contemporaries.

In addition to the West End theatres there are dozens of fine suburban playhouses and about 60 fringe venues, championing new, experimental works. In summer outdoor theatre is popular, too, in venues such as Regent's Park; check the local listings magazines for details.

Music, Opera and Ballet

Top concert venues include the **Royal Festival Hall** *(see page 55)*, with its new improved acoustics, and the **Barbican** *(see page 67)*, home of the London Symphony Orchestra; the **Royal Albert Hall** *(see page 76)* hosts the summer BBC Promenade Concerts (the 'Proms'), while the **Wigmore Hall** *(see page 47)* does chamber recitals. Lunchtime concerts are held in churches including Westminster's **St John's**, **Smith Square** (tel: 020 7222 1061) and **St Martin-in-the-Fields** *(see page 26)* and Piccadilly's **St James's** *(see page 46)*.

London's main venues for opera are Covent Garden's **Royal Opera House** *(see page 42)*, where ballet is also performed, and the **Coliseum** (tel: 020 7632 8300; <www.eno.org>), home of the English National Opera (performances in English), in St Martin's Lane. For modern dance, try the capital's leading venue, **Sadler's Wells Theatre** *(see page 80)*.

Jazz venues include **Ronnie Scott's** (47 Frith Street, tel: 020 7439 0747; <www.ronniescotts.co.uk>), **Jazz Café** (5 Parkway, Camden, tel: 0870 060 3777; <www.meanfiddler.com>) and the **Pizza Express Jazz Club** (10 Dean Street; tel: 020 7734 3220; <www.pizzaexpress.co.uk>).

The popularity of rock venues waxes and wanes. The latest shows are fully covered in *Time Out (see page 117)*.

Nightlife

London is a great place to party, with hundreds of bars and clubs offering an eclectic range of music to a diverse clientele. Soho has long been central to London's mainstream nightlife and gay

A Champagne cocktail

scene, and still has plenty of great bars, as long as you steer clear of Leicester Square. Shoreditch and Hoxton (near Old Street tube station) draw trendy crowds, and the rich and famous party in the exclusive clubs of Mayfair and Kensington. Camden is the place to go for indie and rock music, and Brixton has a range of partying options as diverse as the area itself. Superclubs such as Fabric (in Farringdon) and Ministry of Sound (in Elephant and Castle) attract top international DJs.

Most clubs don't get going until 10pm or 11pm; some run until public transport starts again in the morning. The downside may be getting home, as public transport is poor after 12.30am (night buses only), and cabs are expensive.

Cinema

Many central London cinemas, especially on Leicester Square, are chains showing new releases on big screens. Alternatives include the South Bank's **National Film Theatre** *(see page 55)*, which hosts the London Film Festival and runs themed seasons of films, the **Prince Charles** (Leicester Place; tel: 0901 272 7007; <www.princecharlescinema.com>) and the **Curzon Mayfair** (tel: 0871 703 3989; <www.curzoncinemas.com>) and **Curzon Soho** (tel: 0871 703 3988). Linked to the NFT is the big-screen IMAX cinema at Waterloo *(see page 54)*.

The boat race

One of London's most famous sporting events is the Easter University Boat Race, during which rowers from Oxford and Cambridge universities race along the Thames from Putney to Mortlake.

SPORTS

The British have always been a sporty race, and Londoners are no exception. There's horse riding and boating in Hyde Park, swimming at Hampstead Heath and sailing at Docklands. Many of London's parks offer cheap public tennis courts. The English Golf Union (<www.english golfunion.org>; tel: 015 2635 4500) has details of driving ranges and golf courses.

The **football** season runs from August to May, with matches usually held on Saturday and Sunday afternoons. The top London clubs are: Arsenal (Emirates Stadium; tel: 020 7704 4242), Chelsea (Stamford Bridge; tel: 0871 984 1905) and Tottenham Hotspur (White Hart Lane; tel: 0844 499 5000). The new Wembley Stadium (<www.wembleystadium. com>), hosts the FA Cup final and national games.

Rugby is played from September to April/May. Top

Skating past the Albert Memorial

Rugby Union games are played at Twickenham Rugby Football Ground (Rugby Road; tel: 0870 405 2000).

Cricket is played in summer at the Oval (Kennington, SE11; tel: 020 7582 7764) and Lord's (St John's Wood, NW8; tel: 020 7616 8500). Buy tickets in advance for Test Matches.

Wimbledon is the venue for the famous two-week annual tennis championship in June/July. Seats for Centre Court and Courts 1 and 2 should be reserved six months in advance. However, you can queue on the day for outside court tickets, and you may be able to buy cheap returns in the afternoon. For information contact the All England Tennis Club (tel: 020 8944 1066; <www.wimbledon.org>).

A carousel in Covent Garden

CHILDREN

London's parks and attractions guarantee youngsters a fun time. Animal-loving kids will enjoy a visit to **London Zoo** *(see page 49)* or the **London Aquarium** *(see page 52)*, while celebrity-spotters should visit **Madame Tussaud's** *(see page 48)*. The latter has a chamber of horrors, and if that appeals to the kids, so should the **London Dungeon** *(see page 62)*. Children can clamber over the old buses and trams at the **London Transport Museum** *(see page 40)*, while the **Natural History Museum** and **Science Museum** *(see pages 73 and 74)* are both good for budding scientists. The **Tower of London** *(see page 69)* enlivens history thanks to Beefeaters with traditional costumes and stories to tell.

London has two toy museums, although they may appeal more to the adults in the group. The **Bethnal Green Museum of Childhood** (Cambridge Heath Road; tel: 020 8983 5200; <www.vam.ac.uk/moc>; open daily 10am–5.45pm; free) is the largest public collection of dolls' houses, games and puppets on view in the world. On a smaller scale is **Pollock's Toy Museum** (<www.pollockstoymuseum.com>).

For toys to take home as gifts, shop at the vast **Hamleys** in Regent Street. **Harrods** is also fun for children and even has a pets' department. Covent Garden is excellent for small, quality craft and toy shops, and the buskers here will keep the whole family amused.

Last, but not least, a ride on the **London Eye** *(see page 53)* is an exciting way to spend half an hour.

Calendar of Events

January New Year's Day (Jan 1): London parade.

February Chinese New Year: celebrations in Soho's Chinatown (centring on Gerrard Street), including traditional lion dances.

March/April Oxford versus Cambridge University Boat Race: the mighty institutions battle it out on the Thames from Putney to Mortlake.

April London Marathon (second or third Sun): the world's largest marathon, with over 30,000 runners raising huge sums for charity.

May Chelsea Flower Show (third or fourth week): the most prestigious annual gardening exhibition in the world.

June Royal Ascot Races: horse races where the upper classes show off their new hats. Trooping the Colour (Sat nearest June 11): the Queen inspects the troops at her official birthday parade. All England Lawn Tennis Championships (late June/early July): the world's greatest tennis players compete for the Wimbledon title.

July–September Henry Wood Promenade Concerts, known as the 'Proms': classical music concerts for eight weeks at the Royal Albert Hall.

August Notting Hill Carnival (bank holiday weekend): huge Caribbean street party around Ladbroke Grove and Portobello Road.

September Great River Race (Sat in early to mid-Sept): hundreds of traditional boats race from Richmond to Greenwich.

October Trafalgar Day Parade (Sun nearest Oct 21): celebrates Lord Nelson's sea victory over Napoleon.

November State Opening of Parliament: watch the Queen and royal procession en route to re-open Parliament after the summer recess. Lord Mayor's Show (second Sat): a popular pageant of carnival floats and the newly elected Lord Mayor in procession from the Guildhall to the Law Courts. Guy Fawkes' Day (Nov 5): fireworks displays and bonfires across the city, commemorating the failed attempt to blow up Parliament. Christmas lights switched on in Oxford and Regent streets.

December Christmas tree and carols in Trafalgar Square: choirs sing nightly beneath the giant tree, presented every year by the people of Oslo. New Year's Eve: celebrations in Trafalgar Square and by the Thames.

EATING OUT

Although London's restaurants are expensive by many people's standards, reflecting the high cost of living here, eating out in the British capital has never been so good. The city has some 12,000 restaurants, and you can eat nachos and noodles, tapas and tempura, balti and bhajis; you can try pizza with Japanese toppings, choose from nearly 200 Thai restaurants or even eat English, a privilege reserved until a few years ago for diners at greasy-spoon cafés, the last remaining eel-and-pie shops and Simpson's in the Strand.

Riverside dining

Ethnic restaurants – especially Indian – provide some of the best-value meals in town, and pubs and wine bars can provide a range of culinary delights, from organic gastro cuisine to good-value snacks. On the whole, London is also a good place to eat out as a vegetarian, with its varied restaurants offering a much better choice of non-meat foods than most European cities.

The main concentration of restaurants is in the West End, with the biggest variety in Soho; many restaurants in Covent Garden offer good-value, pre-show suppers, due to the concentration of theatres in that area. Upmarket

Kensington, Chelsea and Notting Hill are home to numerous designer restaurants, while the City has many oyster bars and big-budget restaurants, aimed at the business luncher, though this area becomes a ghost town at the weekends.

A selection of recommended restaurants is included at the end of this guide *(see page 132)*.

Traditional fish and chips

British Cuisine

The rebirth of formerly stodgy, unimaginative British cuisine is due to a large degree to a new generation of chefs, many of whom drip with Michelin stars. New life has been injected into traditional English recipes by combining them with French and ethnic influences. These creative chefs make the best of top-quality, seasonal ingredients, while also making meals lighter.

For those looking for the most traditional of British food, however, popular dishes include:

Roast Beef. The great traditions of Sunday lunch and roast carveries are still very much alive, and sampling them provides an insight into everyday life in England. However, choose carefully, as there is a huge difference between good and bad versions of these meals.

Fish and Chips. It's surprisingly hard to find this nutritious British dish, traditionally served with mushy peas, cooked freshly to order (as opposed to reheated), but the real thing can be found at Rock & Sole Plaice (47 Endell Street, Covent Garden), Sea Shell (49–51 Lisson Grove, Marylebone) and Geales (2 Farmer Street, Notting Hill).

Pie and Mash. If you want a true taste of the old East End look for a Pie and Mash Shop, where you'll get minced beef pie and mashed potatoes with a unique green sauce called liquor, made from parsley. Eels may also be on the menu. Most Pie and Mash shops are in the East End – the nearest authentic one to the West End is R. Cooke at The Cut, by Waterloo Station.

Puddings. Although not great for slimmers, traditional English desserts – 'puddings' – have a certain charm. Most are filling affairs, such as rib-sticking, steamed jam roly-poly or treacle (molasses) pudding. Slightly lighter are fruit pies and crumbles, with a top crust of crumbly pastry. Puddings are traditionally smothered in 'custard', a sweet, hot, milky sauce.

Breakfast
The traditional full English breakfast consists of fried eggs, bacon, sausage, eggs, tomatoes, beans, mushrooms and per-

Afternoon tea is an English institution

haps toast, all on one plate, served with a cup of tea. At traditional establishments kippers and porridge may also be on the menu. If this sounds a little heavy, don't worry, much lighter fare is nearly always available, from croissants to cereals, as well a range of coffees, take-away or otherwise.

Afternoon Tea

This highly traditional and genteel event takes place in some of the grander hotels at around 3.30pm and consists of thinly cut sandwiches (often cucumber), a variety of cakes and a pot of tea. The brew varies from classic Indian teas such as Assam and Darjeeling to the more flowery Earl Grey. Venues include the Waldorf Hilton (Aldwych; tel: 020 7836 2400), which also has tea dances; the Ritz *(see page 46)*; and the Dorchester (Park Lane; tel: 020 7629 8888).

International Cuisine

Every significant food style in the world is represented in London, from Afghan to Italian, Spanish, Turkish and Vietnamese. The top end is still dominated by the French, though home-grown chefs are making a determined assault with their own brand of 'Modern British' cuisine *(see page 101)*. Indian and Chinese restaurants dominate the ethnic scene, and these can be an excellent lunch-time choice with bargain, fixed-price buffets. Try dim sum (savoury dumplings) in any of Soho's authentic Chinese restaurants during the day. The interest in Asian food has grown so that Thai, Malaysian and Vietnamese restaurants are becoming well established in London. Middle Eastern restaurants are also popular, especially in the Arab neighbourhoods around the Edgware Road.

Pubs and Bars

Like most other things in a city this size, it is impossible to generalise about the 5,000-plus pubs and bars in London.

The Kings Head in Chelsea

There are still plenty of the traditional pubs that London is famous for, oak-panelled and cosy, and proud of the quality of their draught beer. Many, however, have been transformed into 'gastropubs'; they've knocked down walls, made light open spaces and now concentrate on food as much as drinks, encouraged by the recent smoking ban. Alongside these is a plethora of bars, some loud, some glitzy, catering to all drinking tastes.

London has several pubs that date from the 17th century, and many retain the atmosphere of that era. One of the best examples is The George in Southwark's Borough High Street, the only surviving galleried coaching inn in London and now owned by the National Trust. At the other end of the scale are contemporary-styled chain bars and gastropubs. These light, airy, fashionably furnished bars are especially accessible to single drinkers, women and anyone wanting a quiet drink during the daytime. Many offer imaginative modern menus.

Most pubs also serve food, although probably not all day. 'Pub grub' generally refers to food bought over the bar rather than an elaborate restaurant-style meal. The menus available at lunchtime generally provide good value and often include traditional British dishes. Bangers and mash (sausages and mashed potato), a Ploughman's lunch (Cheddar cheese, bread and mixed pickles) and steak and kidney pie are traditional pub grub, although many places now offer more adventurous food, from Caesar salad to lasagne, steak, and pork and chicken options. Most pubs offer at least one vegetarian dish.

What to Drink

The traditional pub drink is English **beer** (ale or bitter), which is drawn up by hand pump and served at the temperature of the cellar; chilling kills it, as beer continues to ferment in the barrel. **Lager** is closer to European and American beers, and should be crisp and refreshing, **stout** is a dark, strong beer (such as Guinness), but many seasoned British drinkers choose **bitter**, a light brown beer that should taste fresh, hoppy, with no fizz, and be served at room temperature. Draught beers are served in pints (just over half a litre) and half pints.

All pubs and bars also stock a range of **wines** – some have excellent wine lists – and **spirits**. **Cocktails** are popular in some of the city's trendier bars. In most London pubs and bars, customers order at the bar and pay immediately, although some bars operate table service.

The minimum age to be served alcohol in Britain is 18. If you have children with you it is worth seeking out pubs with gardens or family rooms (ie without a bar).

Eating and Drinking Hours

In general, breakfast is served 7–11am, lunch from noon–2.30pm, afternoon tea 3–5pm, and dinner 6–11pm. In practice, you can eat whatever you want, when you want, if you know where to look – Soho and Covent Garden have the most options for round-the-clock dining. Although pubs can now apply for 24-hour licenses, most are only open 11am–11pm Mon–Sat (though many stay open a couple of hours later on Fri and Sat) and Sun noon–10.30pm.

HANDY TRAVEL TIPS

An A–Z Summary of Practical Information

A

ACCOMMODATION (see also page 126)

London has everything from grand hotels of international renown to family-run guest houses, self-catering flats and youth hostels. However, bargains are hard to come by, as are affordable hotels right in the centre of the city. The main concentrations are around Victoria, Earl's Court/Kensington, the West End and Bayswater. The Bloomsbury area (WC1) is a clever choice, as it's central, characterful and has accommodation at reasonable prices.

Almost all hotels offer special deals that are cheaper than the published 'rack rate', particularly at weekends and outside peak season, so it is always worth checking. It's important to book ahead, as London fills up in the summer (May and September are particularly crowded because of conference traffic), but if you arrive without a reservation, head for a Tourist Information Centre *(see page 123)*. The London Tourist Board operates an efficient room-booking service.

Rooms must usually be vacated by midday on the day of departure.

AIRPORTS

London is served by five airports: the two major hubs are Heathrow and Gatwick, while Stansted, Luton (both north of the centre) and London City are primarily for chartered, budget or short-haul flights.

Heathrow (tel: 0870 0000 123; <www.heathrowairport.com>) can be daunting – the walk to the central building from an international gate can seem to take forever. The fastest connection from the airport to central London is the Heathrow Express to Paddington Station, which runs every 15 minutes and takes 15 minutes. The fare is a hefty £15.50 single (£14.50 online) – possibly the world's costliest rail ticket per mile. Paddington is on the District, Circle, Bakerloo and Hammersmith and City Underground lines. Heathrow Connect run a cheaper service that takes 30 minutes and costs £6.90.

There is also a direct Underground route (£4 single), on the Piccadilly Line, which reaches the West End in around 40 minutes. It goes directly to Kensington, Knightsbridge, Piccadilly, Covent Garden and Bloomsbury (Russell Square) and operates from 5am (6am on Sunday) until 11.50pm (11.30pm on Sunday).

National Express (tel: 08705 808080; <www.nationalexpress.com> run buses roughly every 15 minutes from 4.55am–9.35pm, from Heathrow Central to Victoria Coach Station. The journey takes approximately 50 minutes and costs £4 (adult one-way).

Heathrow is also well-served for taxis; a ride into town in a familiar London 'black cab' (licensed taxi) will cost from £30 plus tip, depending on destination.

Gatwick (tel: 0870 000 2468; <www.gatwickairport.com>) is 27 miles (43km) south of London. The airport isn't on the Underground network, but it has sophisticated train and coach services into London, running to and from Victoria Station. The Gatwick Express leaves every 15 minutes from 3.30am and 12.30am Victoria to Gatwick and 4.35am–1.35am Gatwick to Victoria. The train takes 30 minutes and costs £16.90 one-way (£28.80 return). Gatwick Express Information Line, tel: 0845 850 1530.

South Eastern Trains run rail services direct from Gatwick to Central London. Journey time is 35–50 minutes, and the fare is considerably less than the Gatwick Express. First Capital Connect runs trains from four London stations: King's Cross, Farringdon, Blackfriars and London Bridge. Journey time to London Bridge is 30–45 minutes.

National Express coaches leave from both the North and South terminals regularly and take around 1 hour 30 minutes to reach Victoria. A single fare for one adult is £6.60 (more on a Fridays).

Stansted (tel: 0870 0000 303; <www.stanstedairport.com>), designed by Sir Norman Foster, is a modern complex 34 miles (54km) northeast of London. The Stansted Express (tel: 08457 484950) leaves for Liverpool Street station every 15 minutes between 5.30am and midnight, then at 12.30am, 1am and 1.30am, and costs £15 each way; the journey takes around 45 minutes. The National Express A6 Coach (tel: 0870 574 7777) leaves for Victoria Station around every 30 minutes, all day, every day, takes around 1 hour 30 minutes and costs £15 return, £10 one way. Taxis will cost about £50 or more.

London City Airport (tel: 020 7646 0000; <www.londoncityairport. com>) connects to destinations in Europe and is mainly used by business commuters. The airport is just 6 miles (10km) east of the City and the best way to reach it is on the Docklands Light Railway. The journey from Bank Underground station in the City to the airport costs £3 and takes around 25 minutes. Alternatively, taxis to the City will cost around £20.

B

BUDGETING FOR YOUR TRIP

In general, London is a very expensive city, so come prepared with a high budget. The following are given as a rough guide only:

Accommodation. Double room with a bath in Central London, excl. breakfast, incl. VAT: £60 to over £300 per night.

Meals and drinks. For a decent English breakfast, expect to pay anywhere from £6 and up, for a Continental breakfast £3 and up; for lunch (in a pub, including one drink) £6–10; for dinner (three courses, including wine, at a reasonable restaurant) £25–40. A bottle of house wine costs £10–15, a pint of beer £3; a coffee £1–2.50.

Entertainment. A ticket to the cinema will cost around £8–12; admission to a club: £5–15. Admission to museums and art galleries is from £4–12 per adult, with children usually half-price.

Transport. A one-day, off-peak Travelcard on the Underground (zones 1 and 2): £5.30. Single bus fare (flat amount across London): £2 (90p with an Oyster card, *see page 120*). You will spend much more if you use taxis.

C

CAR HIRE (see also DRIVING)

Heavy traffic, a lack of parking and the congestion charge mean that a car is generally more of a hindrance than a help in central London, so only rent one if you want to explore further afield. All the global car-rental companies are represented in London; most have outlets at the airports as well as in the centre. Weekly hire rates start at around £200. The following are members of the London Tourist Board: **Europcar**, tel: 0870 607 5000; **Hertz Rentacar**, tel: 020 7026 0077; **Avis**, tel: 0870 6060100.

To rent a car, you must be at least 21 years old and be in possession of a valid driving licence (held for at least one year) and a credit card. The cost usually includes insurance and unlimited free mileage but does not include insurance cover for accidental damage to interior trim, wheels and tyres or insurance for other drivers without prior approval. Some companies offer special weekend and holiday rates.

CLIMATE

The English are famous for their preoccupation with the weather – a fascination largely due to the British climate's unpredictable nature. The weather in the capital is generally mild compared with that in the rest of the country. The summers of 2003 and 2006 were

	J	F	M	A	M	J	J	A	S	O	N	D
°C	6	7	10	13	17	20	22	22	19	14	10	7
°F	43	45	50	55	63	68	72	72	66	57	50	45

unexpectedly tropical, but good weather is certainly not guaranteed; likewise, extremely cold weather and snow are rare.

CLOTHING

London is best approached with layers of clothing, as the weather can change within the course of a couple of days. While the city's reputation for rain may be somewhat exaggerated, you should pack an umbrella just in case. Fairly casual clothes are acceptable everywhere but classier restaurants and pickier nightclubs.

COMPLAINTS

If your complaint is against a tourist attraction and you can't resolve it with the manager, contact the nearest Tourist Information Centre *(see page 123)*. If you're unhappy with a purchase, you have the right to return it as long as you have the receipt and original packaging. If the shop refuses, or you have any other problem involving overcharging or bad workmanship, appeal to the Citizens Advice Bureau (CAB); call directory enquiries *(see page 122)* for the number of the local CAB office.

CRIME AND SAFETY

Hold on to your purse and put your wallet in a breast pocket in public. Be on your guard after dark away from crowded streets and in the Underground. Use only legitimate minicabs and black cabs.

In an emergency, dial 999 from any telephone (no money or card required). Otherwise telephone the nearest police station, listed under 'Police' in the telephone directory.

CUSTOMS AND ENTRY REQUIREMENTS

To enter the UK, you need a valid passport (or any form of official identification if a citizen of the European Union). Commonwealth citizens, Americans, EU nationals or citizens of most other European and South American countries don't need visas.

There are no official restrictions on the movement of goods within the European Union, if those goods were bought within the EU. However, British Customs have these personal-use 'guide levels': tobacco: 3,200 cigarettes, 400 cigarillos, 200 cigars, 3kg tobacco; alcohol: 10 litres spirits, 20 litres fortified wines, 90 litres wine, 110 litres beer.

Those entering from a non-EU country are subject to these limits: tobacco: 200 cigarettes or 100 cigarillos or 50 cigars or 250g of tobacco; alcohol: 1 litre of spirits, or 2 litres of fortified or sparkling wine, or 2 litres of table wine (an additional 2 litres of wine if no spirits are bought); 60cc perfume, 250cc eau de toilette. There are no restrictions on the amount of currency you can bring into the country.

D

DRIVING (see also CAR HIRE)

If you're only staying a short while in the Greater London area, and are unfamiliar with the geography of the capital, don't hire a car. Negotiating Central London in a car is highly stressful, owing to the city's web of one-way streets, bad signposting and impatient drivers.

If a car is a necessity, you should drive on the left and observe speed limits (police detection cameras are numerous). It is illegal to drink and drive, and penalties are severe. Drivers and passengers must wear seat belts – failure to do so can result in a fine. For further information on driving in Britain consult a copy of the *Highway Code*.

Breakdown. The following organisations operate 24-hour breakdown assistance: AA, tel: 0800 887 766; RAC, tel: 0800 828 282. Phone calls to these numbers are free (except from mobiles), but the service is free to members only.

Congestion charge. Cars driving into a clearly marked Congestion Zone, extending between Kensington and the City, between 7am and 6pm Mon–Fri are filmed, and their owners are fined if a payment of

£8 has not been made by midnight the same day (or £10 the following day). You can pay at many small shops, including newsagents, by phone (tel: 0845 900 1234) or at <www.cclondon.com>.

Fuel. Petrol (gasoline) is sold at garages and outside many supermarkets (priced in litres).

Parking. This is a big problem in congested central London. Meters are slightly less expensive than NCP (multi-storey) car parks, but only allow parking for a maximum of two hours; it can also be hard to find a free one. Do not leave your car parked on a meter a moment longer than your time allows and do not return and insert more money once your time has run out – both are finable offences. Most meter parking is free after 6.30pm daily and after 1.30pm in most areas on Saturday and all day Sunday; however, always check this on the meter.

Speed limits. Unless otherwise indicated these are: 30mph (50km/h) in urban areas, 60mph (100km/h) on normal roads away from built-up areas, 70mph (112km/h) on motorways and dual carriageways.

E

ELECTRICITY

The standard current in Britain is 240 volt, 50 cycle AC. Plugs have three pins rather than two, so bring an adaptor as necessary.

EMBASSIES AND CONSULATES

Australia: Australia House, Strand, WC2B 4LA, tel: 020 7379 4334.
Canada: Macdonald House, 1 Grosvenor Square, W1K 4AB, tel: 020 7258 6600.
Ireland: 17 Grosvenor Place SW1X 7HR, tel: 020 7235 2171.
New Zealand: 80 Haymarket, SW1Y 4TQ, tel: 020 7930 8422.
US: 24 Grosvenor Square, W1A 1AE, tel: 020 7499 9000.

EMERGENCIES

For police, fire brigade or ambulance dial 999 from any telephone (no money or card required) and tell the operator which service you require.

G

GAY AND LESBIAN TRAVELLERS

The gay scene in London centres around Soho, Earl's Court and Vauxhall, with Old Compton Street in Soho offering specialist bookstores, bars and shops. For information call the Lesbian and Gay Switchboard on 020 7837 7324. *Time Out (see page 117)* has listings for gay venues.

GETTING TO LONDON

By Air. There are regular flights from most major airports in the world to London. For information on the city's airports, *see page 107*.

By Eurostar/Le Shuttle. The Channel Tunnel provides Eurostar passenger services by rail from Paris Nord and Brussels Midi to London St Pancras. For further details, visit <www.eurostar.com> or tel: 08705 186186 in the UK, or outside UK, tel: +44 (0)1233 617 575.

Vehicles are carried by train through the tunnel from Folkestone in Kent to Nord-Pas de Calais in France by Le Shuttle. Bookings are not essential, but advisable at peak times. Fares vary according to the time of travel: late at night or in the early morning is cheapest.

By Ferry. Sea services operate between 12 British and over 20 Continental ports. The major ferries have full facilities and for people arriving by boat there is a sense of occasion that can never be matched by an underground train. The shortest ferry crossing time from the Continent is about 1 hour 30 minutes, from Calais to Dover, which is approximately 2 hours from London by train.

P&O (<www.poferries.com>; UK tel: 0871 664 5645) sails to Dover from Calais; to Portsmouth from Bilbao in Spain; and to Hull from Zeebrugge in Belgium and Rotterdam in the Netherlands. **Seafrance** (<www.seafrance.com>; UK tel: 0871 663 2546) also runs ferries from Calais to Dover. **Brittany Ferries** (<www.brittany-ferries.co.uk>; UK tel: 0870 907 6103) sails to Portsmouth from St Malo, Cherbourg and Caen; to Poole in Dorset from Cherbourg; and to Plymouth from Roscoff in France and Santander in Spain. **Stena Line** (<www.stenaline.co.uk>; UK tel: 08705 707070) sails from the Hook of Holland to Harwich in Essex.

By Coach. National Express run coaches between London and around 25 other countries in Europe. For information and booking visit <www.nationalexpress.com> or tel: 08705 808080.

GUIDED TOURS

Bus tours. For a good introduction to the sights of London, take a tour on a double-decker bus with an English-speaking guide or taped commentary. Departure points include Marble Arch, Trafalgar Square or London Bridge. Most tickets allow you to hop on and off at various points. Operators include the Big Bus Company (tel: 020 7233 9533) and the Original London Sightseeing Tour (tel: 020 8877 1722).

Walking tours. These are an ideal way of getting to know London in the company of a qualified guide. London Walks (tel: 020 7624 3978) has almost 100 walks, many with literary and historical themes. Other operators include Secret London Walks and Visits (tel: 020 8881 2933) and City of London Walks (<www.cityoflondon walks.co.uk>).

Black Taxi Tours. These offer a full commentary from knowledgeable cabbies. Tours are two hours long. Cost £90 per cab – up to five passengers. For 24-hour booking, tel: 020 7935 9363.

River travel. Much of London's history is centred on the Thames, and seeing the city from the river provides a fascinating perspective. City Cruises (tel: 020 7740 0400) serve the main piers down to Tower Pier and Greenwich; Thames River Services (tel: 020 7930 4097) run from Westminster Pier to Greenwich.

Canal trips. Jason's Trip (tel: 020 7286 3428) is a traditional painted narrow boat making 90-minute trips along the Regent's Canal between Little Venice and Camden Lock, Apr–Oct. The London Waterbus Company (tel: 020 7482 2660) runs from Camden Lock to Little Venice, with discounted tickets to the zoo at Regent's Park.

H

HEALTH AND MEDICAL CARE

EU citizens can receive free treatment on producing a European Health Insurance Card. Citizens of other countries must pay, except for emergency treatment (always free). Major hospitals include Charing Cross Hospital (Fulham Palace Road, W6, tel: 020 8846 1234) and St Thomas's (Lambeth Palace Road, SE1, tel: 020 7188 7188). Guy's Hospital Dental Department is at St Thomas Street, SE1, tel: 020 7188 9282. For the nearest hospital or doctor's, ring NHS Direct, tel: 0845 46 47. **Late pharmacies:** Boots on Piccadilly Circus and Bliss Chemist at 5 Marble Arch stay open till midnight.

L

LEFT LUGGAGE

Most of the main railway stations have left-luggage departments where you can leave your suitcases on a short-term basis, although all are extremely sensitive to potential terrorist bombs. To check whether a station has a left-luggage desk, call National Rail Enquiries, tel: 08457 484950.

LOST PROPERTY

If you leave anything on a bus, tube or taxi, ask in person at the London Transport Lost Property Office, 200 Baker Street (open Mon–Fri 8.30am–4pm; tel: 0845 330 9882; <www.tfl.gov.uk>), near Baker Street Underground station.

M

MAPS

Free maps of London are available from Tourist Information Centres *(see page 123)*. Free Underground maps are available from Tube stations, while free bus route maps are available at bus stations. The *London A–Z*, an invaluable streetplan of the city centre and suburbs, is available in a range of sizes from newsagents and bookshops.

MEDIA

Newspapers. National papers include the *Daily Telegraph* and *The Times* (on the right politically), *The Independent* (in the middle) and *The Guardian* (left of centre). Most have Sunday equivalents. The *Financial Times* is dominant in its field. Except for the *Daily Mirror*, the tabloids (*The Sun, Star, Daily Mail, Daily Express* and *Metro*) are conservative. The *Evening Standard* (Mon–Fri) is good for cinema and theatre listings. Foreign papers are sold at many news-stands and main railway stations.

Listings magazines. Most comprehensive is the weekly *Time Out*; *Metro*, out Monday to Friday, is also good. The paper available free at Underground stations, and confusingly also named *Metro*, similarly has arts and events listings.

Television. BBC1 and BBC2 are financed by annual TV licences; ITV, Channel 4 (C4) and Five are funded by advertising. There are scores of cable and satellite channels.

Radio. BBC stations include Radio 1 (98.8 FM, pop), Radio 2 (89.1 FM, easy listening), Radio 3 (91.3 FM, classical music), Radio 4 (93.5 FM, current affairs, plays), Radio 5 Live (909 AM, news and sport) and BBC London (94.9 FM, music, chat). Commercial stations include Capital FM (95.8 FM, pop) and Classic FM (100.9 FM).

MONEY

Currency. The monetary unit is the pound sterling (£), divided into 100 pence (p). Banknotes: £5, £10, £20, £50. Coins: 1p, 2p, 5p, 10p, 20p, 50p, £1, £2. Many of London's large stores also accept euros.

Banks. Most banks open 9.30am–4.30pm Monday to Friday, with Saturday morning banking common in shopping areas. Major English banks tend to offer similar exchange rates, so it's only worth shopping around if you have large amounts of money to change. Banks charge no commission on sterling travellers cheques, and if a London bank is affiliated to your own bank, it will not charge for cheques in other currencies either. You will need ID such as a passport to change travellers cheques.

ATMS. You will probably get the best rate by using an ATM, known as a cashpoint or cash machine, with your bank card from home. There are hundreds of cash machines across London, inside and outside banks, in supermarkets and at rail and Underground stations. They operate on global credit and debit systems including Maestro/Cirrus, Switch, Visa and others.

Credit cards. International credit cards are almost universally accepted in shops, restaurants, hotels etc. Signs on display at the entrance or next to the till should confirm which cards are accepted.

Currency exchange. Post offices and Marks and Spencer have *bureaux de change* that don't charge commission. Some high-street travel agents, such as Thomas Cook, operate *bureaux de change* at good rates. At private *bureaux de change* (some open 24 hours), rates can be very low and commissions high. If you have to use one, check it has a London Tourist Board code of conduct sticker. Chequepoint is a reputable chain with branches at Gloucester Road and Marble Arch.

Tax refunds for tourists. A sales tax called Value Added Tax (VAT), currently 17.5 percent, is levied on most shop goods in Britain. Non-European visitors may claim this back, when spending over a certain amount. A VAT-refund form, available from retailers, needs to be completed and shown to customs, along with all relevant goods and receipts. Ask in shops or at the airport for full details.

O

OPENING HOURS

Banks: Usually Mon–Fri 9.30am–4.30pm, although some close at 3.30pm. Some banks open for limited services on Saturday mornings.
Museums: Mon–Sat 10am–5 or 6pm, and Sun from 2 or 2.30–5 or 6pm. Some museums open earlier on Sundays; some (notably the major ones) also offer late-night viewing at least once a week.
Offices: Mon–Fri 9 or 9.30am–5 or 5.30pm.
Pubs: Most pubs open Mon–Sat 11am–11pm, Sun noon–10.30pm.
Shops: Mon–Sat 9 or 9.30am–5.30 or 6pm. Many central London shops open on Sun for up to six hours, some time between 10am and 6pm. Late-night shopping nights are Wed till 7pm in Chelsea and Knightsbridge, Thurs till 7.30 or 8pm on Oxford and Regent streets.

P

POLICE

Police, identifiable by their black uniforms and high-rise hats, are usually unarmed and, on the whole, friendly. For emergencies, tel: 999.

POST OFFICES

Most post offices open Mon–Fri 9am–5.30pm and Sat 9am–noon. Stamps are sold at post-office counters, machines outside post offices and a variety of shops (newsagents, supermarkets etc), indicated by a red 'stamps' sign. There is a two-tier service: first-class should reach a UK destination the next day, second-class will take at least a day longer. A first-class stamp within the UK for a letter up to 20gm costs 34p (within Europe: 48p). London's main post office (open Mon–Sat 8am–8pm) is at 24–8 William IV Street, near Trafalgar Square.

PUBLIC HOLIDAYS

On public (or 'bank') holidays, banks and offices close, but most other amenities remain open. They are: New Year's Day (January 1), Good Friday, Easter Monday, May Day (first Monday in May), Spring Bank Holiday (last Monday in May), Summer Bank Holiday (last Monday in August), Christmas Day and Boxing Day (December 25 and 26).

PUBLIC TRANSPORT

For information on buses, underground, DLR and trains contact Transport for London (<www.tfl.gov.uk>, tel: 020 7222 1234). For national rail queries, tel: 08457 484950.

Oyster cards. These allow holders to obtain significant discounts (often 50 percent or more) on bus, DLR and Tube travel. They are available from Tube stations, Travel Information Centres and some newsagents for a refundable £3 deposit. You pay to put credit on the card; this is then used to pay for journeys by touching the card against a yellow reader.

Underground. Known colloquially as the Tube, this is the quickest way to get across town. However, it badly needs investment, and in the rush hours (8am–9.30am and 5–6.30pm) stations and trains are packed with commuters. Services run 5.30am–12.30am (Sun until 11.30pm). If you're heading for the end of a line, your last train may leave closer to 11pm.

Make sure you have a valid ticket and keep it after you have passed it through the electronic barrier – you will need it to exit at your destination. Tube maps are available free at Underground stations. Note that some lines split into two, so always check the front of the train and, if there is one, the electronic destination board, to ensure that the train is going in the right direction.

Stations are split into six zones, depending on location, and fares are charged accordingly (a single journey in zone 1 costs £4, or £1.50 with an Oyster card off peak). A one-day Travelcard offers unlimited use of buses, DLR, tubes and trains; a card for zones 1 and 2 is £5.30 off-peak (not valid before 9.30am) or £6.80, peak. A 7-day card (with passport-style photograph) costs £24.20 (zones 1 and 2).

Docklands Light Railway (DLR). This is one of the best (and cheapest) ways to see the old but revived docks area. The fully automated service runs east from Bank and Tower Hill Tube stations to Beckton, London City Airport and Stratford. A branch also goes south to Canary Wharf, Greenwich and Lewisham, in southeast London. The railway operates like the Tube, with similar fares. Some of the views along the routes are superb.

Buses. Most buses run from 6am–11 or 11.30pm and are then supplemented by night buses, which run roughly every hour till dawn and usually start at Trafalgar Square. The flat adult fare across London is £2 if you pay on the bus, £1 per ticket if you use a £6 'saver' book, or 90p with an Oyster card. On some lines you must buy your ticket in advance from a ticket machine at the bus stop.

Trains. London's principal mainline (as opposed to Underground) stations are Euston, King's Cross, Liverpool Street, Paddington, St

Pancras, Victoria and Waterloo. If you are staying in the suburbs, the fastest way into central London is often by this network, used heavily by commuters but relatively quiet between rush hours.

Non-British residents who intend travelling around the country might wish to buy a BritRail Pass (<www.britrail.com>), which allows unlimited travel for certain periods (sold outside Britain only).

T

TAXIS

Official black cabs are licensed and display the regulated charges on the meter. You can hail a cab if its yellow light is on. You can also call for a black cab (Radio Taxis, tel: 020 7272 0272; Dial-a-Cab, tel: 020 7253 5000) but you will be charged for the time and miles it takes to pick you up as well as the journey itself.

Licensed minicabs can only be hired by telephone, so avoid any illegal ones touting for business late at night (this is common practice in central London, where black cabs can be scarce). Good, licensed minicab firms include Addison Lee (tel: 020 7387 8888).

TELEPHONES

London's UK dialling code is 020. To call from abroad, dial the 44 international access code for Britain, then 20, then the eight-digit number. To phone abroad, dial 00 followed by the international code for the country you want, then the number: Australia (61); Ireland (353); US and Canada (1), etc. If using a US credit phone card, first dial the company's access number as follows: **Sprint**, tel: 0800 917 3105; **MCI**, tel: 0800 890 222; **AT&T**, tel: 0800 890 011.

Operator: 100
International Operator: 155
Directory Enquiries (UK): 118500, 118118 or 118811
International Directory Enquiries: 118505, 118866 or 118899

Despite the ubiquity of mobiles (cellphones), London still has a fair number of public phone boxes; most accept phone cards, which are widely available from post offices and newsagents in amounts from £1 to £20. At coin phone boxes, the smallest coin accepted is 20p.

TIME ZONES

In winter Great Britain is on Greenwich Mean Time. In summer (April–October) clocks are put forward one hour.

TIPPING

Many restaurants automatically add a 10–15 percent service charge to your bill. It's your right to deduct this if you're not happy with the service. It's usual to tip guides, porters and cabbies about 10 percent.

TOILETS

There are usually public conveniences in railway stations, parks and museums. Few Underground stations have toilets for customer use (Piccadilly and the new Jubilee line stations are rare exceptions). There is often, although not always, a charge of 10p or 20p to use public toilets, and you may find that those in pubs or bars are reserved for customer use only. Department stores often have free customer toilets.

TOURIST INFORMATION

The main Britain Visitor Centre, 1 Regent Street, Piccadilly Circus, SW1, no tel; <www.visitbritain.com>, has an accommodation- and theatre-booking service, bookshop and *bureau de change*. There are 15 other Britain Visitor Centres in Greater London.

Information and booking are also available at the London Information Centre in the 'tkts' booth in Leicester Square (open daily 8am–midnight; <www.londoninformationcentre.com>; tel: 020 7292 2333. You can also contact the British Tourist Authority (BTA), Thames Tower, Black's Road, London W6 9EZ, tel: 020 8846 9000, or the following BTA offices:

Australia: Level 2, 15 Blue Street, North Sydney NSW2060, tel: 02 9021 4400.

Canada: 5915 Airport Road, Suite 120, Mississauga, Ontario, L4V1T1, tel: 1-888 VISIT UK.

New Zealand: Level 17, IAG House, 1st Queen Street, PO Box 105–652, Auckland, tel: 9 309 1899.

Singapore: 600 North Bridge Road, #09-10 Parkview Square, Singapore 188778, tel: (65) 6511 4311.

US: Suite 1001, 625 N. Michigan Avenue, Chicago, IL 60611 1977, tel: 312 787 0464. Suite 570, 10880 Wilshire Blvd, Los Angeles, CA 90024, tel: 310 470 2782. Suite 701, 551 Fifth Avenue, New York, NY 10176–0799, tel: 1 800 462 2748.

TRAVELLERS WITH DISABILITIES

The definitive guidebook is *Access in London* by Gordon Couch, William Forrester and David McGaughey (Bloomsbury Publishing ISBN 978-07475-69336). The Visit London website also has information about accessibility: <www.visitlondon.com/maps/accessibility>. For details on public transport get *Getting Around London* from Transport for London's customer services office at 55 Broadway, London SW1M 0BD, and Transport for London's *Tube Access Guide* (free from tube stations).

Artsline is a free telephone information service for disabled people in London, covering the arts and entertainment (tel: 020 7388 2227, <www.artsline.org.uk>), available Mon–Fri 10am–5.30pm.

For information on accommodation visit <www.holidaycare.org.uk> or call the Holiday Care Service helpline on 0845 124 9971.

W

WEBSITES

London has many internet cafés. The most widespread is the Easy-Internet chain <www.easyinternetcafe.com>, which has mega cafés in Victoria, Oxford Street, Trafalgar Square, Tottenham Court Road and Kensington, open 24 hours. Smaller cyber cafés include Webshak in Soho, Cyberia in Whitfield Street, Offshore Café behind Piccadilly Circus in Sackville Street and Waterstone's on Piccadilly.

The following are useful websites giving general information on London for visitors and locals:

www.visitlondon.com London Tourist Board site with information on hotels, restaurants, pubs and attractions

www.thisislondon.co.uk site maintained by the *Evening Standard* newspaper, with detailed listings

www.netlondon.com links to hotels, museums, theatres

www.tfl.gov.uk travel information from Transport for London

www.bbc.co.uk the BBC's vast site; news and listings

WEIGHTS AND MEASURES

This is something of a half-way house. Distances are still measured in miles, and drinks are served as pints, though recent changes in the law mean that all goods must officially be sold in metric.

Y

YOUTH HOSTELS AND YMCAS

The International Youth Hostel Federation (<www.yha.org.uk>) has beds costing from £16 to £25 in these locations: 36–8 Carter Lane, EC4 (tel: 0870 770 5764), near St Paul's; 38 Bolton Gardens, Earl's Court, SW5 (tel: 0870 770 5804); Holland Walk, Kensington, W8 (tel: 0870 770 5866); 14 Noel Street, off Oxford Street, W1 (tel: 0870 770 5984); 20 Salter Road, Thameside, SE16 (tel: 0870 770 6010); and 79–81 Euston Road, St Pancras, NW1 (tel: 0870 770 6044).

YMCAs (<www.ymca.org.uk>) are at 2 Fann Street, Barbican, EC2 (tel: 020 7628 0697); 8 Errol Street, EC1 (tel: 020 7614 5000); and 200 The Broadway, Wimbledon, SW19 (tel: 020 8542 9055).

Recommended Hotels

Rooms in London tend to be small – unless you pay a premium – and prices are high across the board. The hotels listed here, arranged according to area, with districts covered in alphabetical order, are intended to complement the areas of London covered in the Where to Go section of this guide. In these listings the West End area has been divided for clarity into the following: Covent Garden, Strand and Embankment; Mayfair; and Soho. Victoria is a popular hotel location but for value, convenience and character, try Bloomsbury. The price ranges, given as guides only, are for a double room, exclusive of breakfast. Many hotels offer special deals at weekends and outside peak season, so it is always worth checking before paying the rack rate.

£££££	over £300
££££	£200–300
£££	£150–200
££	£100–150
£	under £100

BLOOMSBURY AND MARYLEBONE

The Academy ££ 21 Gower Street, WC1E 6HG, tel: 020 7631 4115, fax: 020 7636 3442; <www.theetoncollection.com>. This delightful boutique hotel is housed within five elegant Georgian townhouses and attempts to recreate for its guests life in 19th-century Bloomsbury (only with all mod cons). The 49 guest rooms are furnished in romantic style in keeping with the architecture, and there are two lovely gardens. Bar and dining room. Complimentary fruit. CD players and music library.

Grange Blooms Hotel £–££ 7 Montague Street, WC1B 5BP, tel: 020 7323 1717, fax: 020 7636 6498; <www.grangehotels.com>. Located very close to the British Museum in the heart of Bloomsbury, this hotel in an 18th-century townhouse has 26 ensuite rooms decorated in traditional style, a pretty paved garden and an attractive dining room.

Sherlock Holmes Hotel ££ *108 Baker Street, W1U 6EG, tel: 020 7034 4830, fax: 020 7958 5211; <www.parkplazasherlockholmes. com>*. Named after the famous sleuth who supposedly lived nearby, this lovely, recently refurbished boutique hotel is well placed for Oxford Street and the West End. The 119 rooms are decorated in a stylish modern take on traditional style.

THE CITY

Andaz Liverpool Street £££££ *40 Liverpool Street, EC2M 7QN, tel: 020 961 1234, fax: 020 961 1235; <www.andaz.com>*. In the heart of the Square Mile, Andaz (formerly the Great Eastern Hotel) offers a new concept in guest services. The ethos is 'casual luxury'; instead of a reception desk, a member of staff will greet you and then look after you throughout your stay. The uber-stylish decor should appeal to both corporate and creative types.

COVENT GARDEN, STRAND, EMBANKMENT

One Aldwych £££££ *1 Aldwych, WC2B 4RH, tel: 020 7300 1000, fax: 020 7300 1001; <www.onealdwych.com>*. Excellently situated a stone's throw from Covent Garden, One Aldwych is the epitome of chic, with high-profile guests to match. Each of 105 rooms has a minimum 6-ft (2-m) wide bed and a television in the bathroom. Amenities include a health club, pool and film-screening room.

The Savoy £££££ *Strand WC2R 0EU, tel: 020 7836 4343, fax: 020 7240 6040; <www.fairmont.com/savoy>*. This large London landmark, set back from the road, has a solid reputation for comfort and personal service, although it is on the formal, traditional side. Closed for £100 million restoration until early 2009.

St Martin's Lane ££££–£££££ *45 St Martin's Lane, WC2N 4HX, tel: 020 7300 5500, fax: 020 7300 5501; <www.stmartinslane.com>*. Designed by Philippe Starck, this Morgans hotel is well established as one of the hippest hotels in London. The 204 minimalist rooms are 'painted' in boldly coloured light. Facilities include the acclaimed Asia de Cuba restaurant and the trendy Light Bar.

Strand Palace Hotel ££ *372 Strand, WC2R 0JJ, tel: 020 7379 4737.* Occupying a central location between Covent Garden and the Thames, and a stone's throw from Trafalgar Square, this is a popular choice for business travellers and tourists. The 785 rooms are decorated in contemporary style.

The Waldorf Hilton ££££–£££££ *Aldwych, WC2B 4DD, tel: 020 7836 2400, fax: 020 7836 7244; <www.hilton.co.uk/waldorf>.* This five-star Edwardian hotel, which dominates Aldwych, has been modernised, and rooms are now in contemporary style. Facilities include a state-of-the-art health club, swimming pool, beauty salon, restaurants, bars and the chic Homage Grand Saloon dining room.

KNIGHTSBRIDGE, KENSINGTON AND CHELSEA

Abbey Court ££ *20 Pembridge Gardens, W2 4DU, tel: 020 7221 7518, fax: 020 7792 0858; <www.abbeycourthotel.co.uk>.* Beautifully restored Notting Hill town house, with the atmosphere of a private home. The 22 rooms have sumptuous Italian marble bathrooms with whirlpool baths.

Berkeley Hotel £££££ *Wilton Place, SW1X 7RL, tel: 020 7235 6000, fax: 020 7235 4330; <www.the-berkeley.co.uk>.* Many rate the sumptuously decorated Berkeley as the best place to stay in London. Facilities include a health suite and pool. Among the restaurants is Gordon Ramsey's Boxwood Café, which has the feel of a sleek, luxury New York café.

Blakes London ££££ *33 Roland Gardens, SW7 3PF, tel: 020 7370 6701, fax: 020 7373 0442; <www.blakeshotel.com>.* This 51-room hotel, slickly designed by Anouska Hempel, is popular among the beautiful people owing to its discreet location, sophisticated service and elegant atmosphere. The original boutique hotel.

Cadogan Hotel £££ *75 Sloane Street, SW1X 9SG, tel: 020 7235 7141, fax: 020 7245 0994; <www.cadogan.com>.* A 65-roomed, 19th-century-style hotel, owned by Stein Hotels and Resorts, in a convenient position between Knightsbridge and Chelsea. It has a history of glamour and scandal – the actress Lily Langtry once lived in what is now the bar and Oscar Wilde was arrested here.

The Gore ££££ *190 Queen's Gate, SW7 5EX, tel: 020 7584 6601, fax: 020 7589 8127; <www.gorehotel.co.uk>*. Idyosyncratic 50-roomed hotel on a quiet street close to the Royal Albert Hall. Every centimetre of the walls seems to be covered in paintings and prints, and the rooms are sumptuous. Popular with a lively, fashionable crowd. The excellent Bistrot 190 is on the ground floor.

Knightsbridge Green Hotel £££ *159 Knightsbridge, SW1X 7PD, tel: 020 7584 6274, fax: 020 7225 1635; <www.thekghotel.co.uk>*. This family-run hotel offers brilliant value for money considering the upmarket area. It's unusual in that it consists mostly of suites, doubles and family-sized rooms. All 28 rooms are non smoking.

Portobello Hotel £££ *22 Stanley Gardens, W11 2NG, tel: 020 7727 2777, fax: 020 7792 9641; <www.portobello-hotel.co.uk>*. A small (24-roomed), extravagantly decorated and painfully hip hotel that includes Julie's restaurant and is particularly popular with movie and rock stars. Kate Moss and Johnny Depp allegedly bathed in champagne here.

Vicarage Hotel £ *10 Vicarage Gate, W8 4AG, tel: 020 7229 4030, fax: 020 8896 9343; <www.londonvicaragehotel.com>*. This is a grand family-run B&B with 18 rooms (few en suite) in a Victorian house overlooking a pleasant garden square in Kensington. The decor is traditional and simple but well maintained. Good value.

MAYFAIR

Brown's Hotel £££££ *30 Albemarle Street, W1S 4BP, tel: 020 7493 6020, fax: 020 7493 9381; <www.brownshotel.com>*. A distinguished, very British, Victorian-style hotel with 117 rooms in a smart Mayfair location. Health club.

Claridge's £££££ *Brook Street, W1K 4HR, tel: 020 7629 8860, fax: 020 7499 2210; <www.claridges.co.uk>*. This London institution with splendid Art Deco reception has long had a reputation for dignity, graciousness and lack of pretension. Lovely central location. Health suite. Restaurants include Gordon Ramsey at Claridge's, headed by the three-Michelin-starred chef.

The Connaught ££££ *16 Carlos Place, W1K 2AL, tel: 020 7499 7070, fax: 020 7314 3542; <www.the-connaught.co.uk>.* Discreet, immaculate service is assured at this sumptuously decorated, if slightly stuffy, hotel. State-of-the-art gym and spa. 124 rooms.

Lanesborough Hotel £££££ *Hyde Park Corner, SW1X 7TA, tel: 020 7259 5599, fax: 020 7259 5606; <www.lanesborough.com>.* The stately Neoclassical facade of the former St George's hospital complements the opulent Regency-style interior of this deluxe hotel overlooking Hyde Park Corner. Despite being a relative newcomer, this is now one of London's finest hotels, and dining includes The Conservatory restaurant.

Metropolitan £££££ *19 Old Park Lane, W1K 1LB, tel: 020 7447 1000, fax: 020 7447 1100; <www.metropolitan.co.uk>.* The Metropolitan's spacious rooms are sleek yet serene, in a successful attempt to recreate a New-York style ambience. The achingly trendy bar is known as a celebrity hangout, and the hotel's restaurant, Michelin-starred Nobu, is equally infamous – both for its legendary black cod and its connections with tennis star Boris Becker.

The Ritz £££££ *150 Piccadilly, W1J 9BR, tel: 020 7493 8181, fax: 020 7493 2687; <www.theritzlondon.com>.* One of the world's most famous hotel names. Everything about the 130-roomed Ritz is the height of opulence – the rooms, decorated with gilding and drapery, are palatial. Tea at the Ritz is an institution *(see pages 46 and 103)*.

Tophams Belgravia £££ *24–32 Ebury Street, SW1W ONY, tel: 020 7730 9469, <www.zolahotels.com>.* Open since 1937, this hotel comprises five converted townhouses and has recently undergone a two-year refurbishment, resulting in a good-value, contemporary boutique hotel offering a full range of guest services.

SOHO

Hazlitt's ££££ *6 Frith Street, W1D 3JA, tel: 020 7434 1771, fax: 020 7439 1524; <www.hazlittshotel.com>.* Spread across three early 18th-century houses in the heart of Soho, elegant Hazlitt's is packed with gorgeous antiques and full of character. Just 23 rooms.

The Regency Hotel £ *19 Nottingham Place, W1U 5LQ, tel: 020 7486 5347, fax: 020 7224 6057; <www.regencyhotelwestend.co.uk>.* An elegantly converted mansion with 20 rooms close to Regent, Oxford and Harley streets. Comfortable accommodation.

THE SOUTH BANK

Premier Travel Inns £ *Central reservations, tel: 0870-242 8000; <www.premiertravelinn.com>.* For value, it's hard to beat Britain's biggest budget hotel chain. There are five Premier Travel Inns in central London but the best-located are at Country Hall and Tower Bridge, on the South Bank. Clean, modern, frill-free accommodation.

TOWER HILL

Tower Thistle Hotel ££££ *St Katherine's Way, E1W 1LD, tel: 0870 333 9106, fax: 0870 333 9206; <www.thistlehotels.com/tower>.* A huge modern hotel on the bank of the Thames, next to the Tower of London, Tower Bridge and handy for the City.

VICTORIA

Elizabeth Hotel £ *37 Eccleston Square, SW1V 1PB, tel: 020 7828 6812, fax: 020 7828 6814; <www.elizabethhotel.com>.* A friendly hotel set in an elegant period square, only two minutes' walk from Victoria Station. 40 rooms, around half with bathrooms.

The Rubens ££££ *39–41 Buckingham Palace Road, SW1W OPS, tel: 020 7834 6600, fax: 020 7958 7725; <www.rubenshotel.com>.* This large, traditional-style hotel is in a smart location by the Royal Mews, very close to Buckingham Palace.

Recommended Restaurants

London is one of the most cosmopolitan cities in the world in which to dine. While it holds its own in terms of top-class restaurants, it also has budget eateries, gastro pubs, ancient inns offering traditional fare, cafés for snacks and a host of restaurants besides. All tastes are catered for, and the selection included here is purely the tip of the iceberg. These restaurants are listed alphabetically, according to location. Price ranges, given as guides only, indicate the cost of a three-course evening meal for one with half a bottle of house wine, including the standard ten percent tip. Lunch menus and set menus may offer better value. To be sure of a table, it's advisable to book in advance – reservations are essential in many of the city's best-known restaurants.

££££	£40 and over
£££	£30–40
££	£20–30
£	less than £20

BLOOMSBURY AND MARYLEBONE

Bertorelli £££ *19–23 Charlotte Street, W1, tel: 020 7636 4174.* Founded in 1913 this branch of Bertorelli now heads a chain of six. Open from breakfast until dinner, and popular for its hospitable bar and simple Italian and bistro food.

Hakkasan ££££ *8 Hanway Place, W1, tel: 020 7927 7000.* Extremely hip basement Chinese restaurant concealed down an alley at the back of Sainsbury's, Tottenham Court Road. Exquisite dim sum (lunch only), exotic and classy fish and meat dishes and delicious puddings. Prices, though, are punishing.

Odin's Restaurant ££££ *27 Devonshire Street, W1, tel: 020 7935 7296.* Grand formal dining room peppered with pictures and antiques, yet good for intimate dinners à deux, as tables are hidden behind old-fashioned screens. Speciality dishes include crab bisque and roast partridge.

Orrery ££££ *55 Marylebone High Street, W1, tel: 020 7616 8000;* *<www.orreryrestaurant.co.uk>*. This beautiful dining room with Art Deco lines above the Marylebone Conran Shop is a mecca for foodies. Stunning, intensely flavoured mains, prize-winning cheese trolley, memorable soufflés and a definitive wine list.

Rasa Samudra £££ *5 Charlotte Street, W1, tel: 020 7637 0222;* *<www.rasarestaurants.com>*. London's first Indian seafood restaurant, offering quality, spicy Keralan seafood and vegetarian dishes in a rambling series of highly decorated townhouse rooms. Another branch on Dering Street, off New Bond Street.

RIBA Café ££ *66 Portland Place, W1, tel: 020 7631 0467; <www. architecture.com>*. Tasty breakfasts and boldly colourful lunches in an appropriately beautiful space provided by the Royal Institute of British Architects. Terrace open in fine weather.

Wagamama £ *4a Streatham Street, WC1, tel: 020 7323 9223;* *<www.wagamama.com>*. Bloomsbury's was the original of a chain which, at last count, was 80 strong. Canteen-like basement with communal tables and bench seating, where staff dish up well-cooked, budget noodles, dumplings, soups and juices.

THE CITY AND EAST LONDON

Angel £ *101 Bermondsey Wall East, SE16, tel: 020 7394 3214*. Built on stilts over the Thames, this pub dates back to the 15th century when monks from the Bermondsey Priory ran it as a tavern. The balcony and upstairs restaurant offer outstanding views of the Thames.

The Eagle £££ *159 Farringdon Road, EC1, tel: 020 7837 1353*. Patronised by journalists from the *Guardian*, whose offices are nearby, the Eagle looks like an ordinary pub from the outside but it does good food including rare steak and a wide range of European beer.

Moro £££ *34–6 Exmouth Market, EC1, tel: 020 7833 8336; <www. moro.co.uk>*. A Spanish-cum-Middle Eastern-cum-North African restaurant on the part shabby, part quirky Exmouth Market, Moro has a reputation for excellent food and service. It has a laid-back feel, the staff are friendly, and dining is unhurried.

Searcy's ££–£££ *Level 2, Barbican, Silk Street, EC2, tel: 020 7588 3008; <www.barbican.org.uk>.* This classy yet relaxed restaurant within the Barbican serves delicious Modern British dishes such as sea trout with fennel and duck with prunes.

Smiths of Smithfield £££ *67–77 Charterhouse Street, EC1, tel: 020 7251 7950 ; <www.smithsofsmithfield.co.uk>.* Brunch on a Saturday or Sunday is really good fun in John Torode's post-industrial complex. Upstairs, a more refined experience is on offer in the restaurant along with views over Smithfield Market.

El Vino ££ *47 Fleet Street, EC4, tel: 020 7353 6786; <www.elvino.co.uk>.* El Vino has long been a favoured local haunt among journalists and politicians and remains hearteningly old-fashioned. Serves British classics (steak and kidney pie, fish and chips, smoked salmon etc) and fabulous wines.

Ye Olde Cheshire Cheese £ *145 Fleet Street, EC4, tel: 020 7353 6170.* Past drinkers at this ancient nooks-and-crannies pub, which dates back to 1667, include Samuel Johnson and Charles Dickens. The restaurant serves established English 'fayre'.

COVENT GARDEN

Belgo Centraal ££ *50 Earlham Street, WC2, tel: 020 7813 2233; <www.belgo-restaurants.co.uk>.* Food revolves around the traditional Belgian mussels and chips but there is plenty more besides, such as fabulous wild boar sausages. A vast list of Belgian beers, waiters dressed as monks plus cool industrial decor.

Le Café Des Amis Du Vin ££ *11–14 Hanover Place, WC2, tel: 020 7379 3444; <www.cafedesamis.co.uk>.* Always crowded, largely due to its location and its reliable French brasserie food with an international flavour. Efficient service. Downstairs is an atmospheric basement bar with a good solid wine list and decent French snacks.

Cork & Bottle £–££ *44–6 Cranbourne Street, WC2, tel: 020 7734 7807.* An excellent retreat from Leicester Square, this casual basement wine bar offers decent food and a notable selection of wines.

Food For Thought £ *31 Neal Street, WC2, tel: 020 7836 0239.* The vegetarian food here is never dull so it gets crowded at lunchtimes, with queues for take-aways. Bring your own wine. Dinner till 8.30pm.

Freud's £ *198 Shaftesbury Avenue, WC2, tel: 020 7240 9933.* At the north end of Neal Street is this funkily decorated basement bunker bar that attracts a trendy crowd. Sometimes has live music.

The Ivy ££££ *1 West Street, WC2, tel: 020 7836 4751; <www.the-ivy.co.uk>.* If you succeed in getting a reservation at this, one of London's most famous haunts (reserve months, rather than days, ahead), you'll enjoy a surprisingly unaffected atmosphere, a familiar menu (predominantly English with international favourites), a strong wine list – and some surreptitious star-spotting (all the celebs seem to dine here).

Lamb and Flag £–££ *33 Rose Street, WC2, tel: 020 7497 9504* Originally known as the 'Bucket of Blood', this characterful timber pub with skewwhiff walls was once a venue for bare-fist boxing.

Rules £££–££££ *35 Maiden Lane, WC2, tel: 020 7836 5314; <www.rules.co.uk>.* London's oldest restaurant, Rules has a traditional menu and beautifully decorated, old-fashioned dining room – think wood panelling and Art Nouveau-style stained glass – to match. It's strong on game, pies, oysters, puddings and real ale.

Sarastro ££ *126 Drury Lane, WC2, tel: 020 7836 0101; <www.sarastro-restaurant.com>.* This restaurant makes for unusual dining with its extraordinary lavish decor and live entertainment (puppet shows and opera). The food is rather more straightforward, although it has a Turkish slant. Value lunch/pre-matinée menus.

Simpsons-in-the-Strand ££££ *100 Strand, WC2, tel: 020 7836 9112; <www.simpsonsinthestrand.co.uk>.* The Grand Divan Tavern is an Edwardian dining room renowned for serving the best roast beef in London. Staunchly traditional and formal, Simpsons is as popular as ever with the English establishment.

KNIGHTSBRIDGE, KENSINGTON AND CHELSEA

The Admiral Codrington £££ *17 Mossop Street, SW3, tel: 020 7581 0005; <www.theadmiralcodrington.co.uk>.* A popular South Kensington pub since the 1960s, the cosy old-fashioned 'Cod' does good, modern European dishes. Bar snacks include homemade soup and fish and chips.

Bibendum ££££ *Michelin House, 81 Fulham Road, SW3, tel: 020 7581 5817; <www.bibendum.co.uk>; <www.conran-restaurants. co.uk>.* Design guru Terence Conran made his name by buying and then restoring buildings of architectural interest, from Michelin House, the former London headquarters of the French tyre company, to Butlers Wharf *(see page 63)*, the **Bluebird** garage *(see below)* and a restored Marylebone stables, **Orrery** *(see page 133)*. Bibendum remains one of his finest creations – if possible, visit on a sunny day, when the light streams through the stained-glass windows. Dishes, which are Modern European, are faultless, the vast wine list impressive, and the service excellent.

Bluebird ££££ *350 King's Road, SW3, tel: 020 7559 1000; <www. danddlondon.com/restaurants>.* Conran's European/Pacific Rim restaurant in a former Chelsea garage is noisy but glamorous, with innovative food. Downstairs is a posh food shop.

Daquise ££ *20 Thurloe Street, SW7, tel: 020 7589 6117.* Central to London's Polish community since World War II. East European food is served in a nice, relaxed, café atmosphere.

Fifth Floor, Harvey Nichols ££££ *109–25 Knightsbridge, SW1, tel: 020 7235 5250; <www.harveynichols.com>.* This elegant restaurant at the top of the department store has an excellent reputation. Patisseries and puddings are made on the day, and starters and main courses are always enticing.

Gordon Ramsay ££££ *68–9 Royal Hospital Road, SW3, tel: 020 7352 4441; <www.gordonramsay.com/ukrestaurants>.* A luxurious setting for the famously short-tempered Michelin-starred chef's wonderful interpretation of French cuisine. He also runs Gordon Ramsay at Claridge's *(see pages 129–30).*

Vingt-Quatre £ *325 Fulham Road, SW10; tel. 020 7376 7224; <www.vingtquatre.co.uk>.* As its name implies, this restaurant serves good hot meals 24 hours hours a day, with a licence to serve alcohol until midnight. It's particularly popular among the trendy, well-heeled Kensington locals.

Zaika £££ *1 Kensington High Street, W8, tel: 020 7795 6533; <www.zaika-restaurant.co.uk>.* Stylish Indian restaurant whose menu incorporates traditional favourites with 'new' Eastern dishes which are both fragrant and subtle. Booking is advised for the set lunch.

MAYFAIR AND ST JAMES'S

L'Autre ££ *5b Shepherd St, W1, tel: 020 7499 4680.* Tucked away in the heart of Shepherd Market *(see page 46),* this quaint half-timbered restaurant offers an odd combination of Polish and Mexican food that works surprisingly well. Romantic atmosphere.

Le Caprice ££££ *Arlington Street, SW1, tel: 020 7629 2239; <www.le-caprice.co.uk>.* Black-and-white, café-style restaurant that is a fashionable place to graze and be seen. Pianist in the evenings. Excellent Sunday brunch.

Criterion Grill £££ *224 Piccadilly, W1, tel: 020 7930 0488.* Possibly the most beautiful restaurant in London, with a gorgeous, high-ceilinged hall decorated with neo-Byzantine mosaics, mirrors and drapes. Chef Marco Pierre White's food is modern French.

Fakhreldine £££ *85 Piccadilly, W1, tel: 020 7493 3424; <www. fakhreldine.co.uk>.* Overlooking Green Park, this is one of London's smartest and most established Middle Eastern restaurants. Fine Lebanese cuisine.

Fortnum and Mason £££ *St James's Restaurant 4th floor, 181 Piccadilly, W1A, tel: 020 7734 8040; <www.fortnumandmason.com>.* The restaurant in this famous food emporium serves cooked breakfasts and excellent roast lunches, as well as its famous afternoon teas.

Le Gavroche ££££ *43 Upper Brook Street, W1, tel: 020 7408 0881; <www.le-gavroche.co.uk>.* Consistently regarded as one of England's top restaurants Le Gavroche was also the first British restaurant to earn three Michelin stars thanks to French chef Albert Roux.

Momo £££ *25–7 Heddon St, W1, tel: 020 7434 4040.* Tucked away behind Regent Street, Momo combines opulent decor with tasty Moroccan cuisine. It has a real party feel in the evening when candles are lit, and the music is upbeat. Also does fabulous cocktails.

Nobu £££ *Metropolitan Hotel, 19 Old Park Lane, W1, tel: 020 7447 4747; <www.noburestaurants.com>.* Celebrity haunt and notoriously hard-to-book, Nobu does sensational Japanese food with a Peruvian twist including its famous black cod in miso. Unfortunately, there are two-hour time limits *(see also page 130)*.

The Ritz Restaurant ££££ *150 Piccadilly, W1, tel: 020 7493 8181; <www.theritzhotel.co.uk>.* Elegant Edwardian restaurant decorated in Louis XVI style. The dining room is sumptuous, but some say that the food could do with improvement, considering the price. Jacket-and-tie dress code.

Veeraswamy ££££ *Victory House, 99 Regent St, W1, tel: 020 7734 1401; <www.veeraswamy.com>.* London's oldest Indian restaurant is brought up-to-date with an adventurous menu combining North and South Indian cooking.

SOHO AND CHINATOWN

Alastair Little £££ *49 Frith Street, W1, tel: 020 7734 5183.* You can rest assured of quality international food at this small Soho restaurant. Its chef namesake no longer mans the stoves, but the cooking remains excellent. Menus are fixed (and good value).

Alphabet Bar £ *61–3 Beak Street, W1, tel: 020 7439 2190*. A very hip Soho hang-out, where the floor of the basement bar is covered by a London street-plan. There's a short, eclectic food menu and drinks range from wine to juices and cocktails. It can get seriously crowded in the evenings.

Andrew Edmunds £££ *46 Lexington Street, W1, tel: 020 7437 5708*. A lack of signage out front gives a secretive feel to this cosy Soho hideaway. Inside, the wood-panelled walls are lit by candle-light. Dishes are simple but varied, ranging from rabbit to pasta.

Bar Italia £ *22 Frith Street, W1, tel: 020 7437 4520*. Retaining its genuine 1950s feel, this is London's most famous Italian bar. No hype, just excellent coffee and an arty, predominately gay crowd. Stays open 24 hours and has a late drinks licence.

Bar du Marché ££ *19 Berwick St W1, tel: 020 7734 4606*. Tucked behind Berwick Street Market, this is a surprisingly unpretentious Soho hangout. Serves a mix of French brasserie-style food, salads and a surprising selection of seafood. Value set menus.

Café Emm £ *17 Frith Street, W1, tel: 020 7437 0723; <www.café emm.com>*. Buzzy, intimate and exceptionally good value, Café Emm stands out for its generous portions, especially given its prime Soho location. The broad menu ranges from calamari to lamb shank. Friendly service.

French House £££ *49 Dean Street, W1, tel: 020 7437 2477*. During the war, this building was a meeting place for members of the French Resistance. Nowadays, there's a bohemian drinking hole downstairs and it's always packed. The wood-panelled restaurant upstairs has a lovely old-fashioned feel and serves traditional French-style dishes typified by rich, wine-based sauces and dark meats. Excellent wine list.

Fung Shing £ *15 Lisle Street, WC2, tel: 020 7437 1539; <www.fung shing.co.uk>*. Has long been one of the best Chinatown restaurants and consequently is always packed. Some original dishes with particularly good fish.

Gay Hussar ££ *2 Greek Street, W1, tel: 020 7437 0973.* A long menu of mouth-watering dishes, such as wild cherry soup, ensure this established Hungarian restaurant of its popularity.

Harbour City £ *46 Gerrard Street, W1, tel: 020 7439 7120.* This is an excellent, reasonably priced restaurant in the middle of Chinatown. With its traditional wood-framed decor and great window table overlooking Gerrard Street, it feels civilised and welcoming. Dim sum (served Mon–Sat until 5pm) dominates the menu.

Meza ££–£££ *100 Wardour Street, W1, tel: 020 7314 4002; <www.conran-restaurants.co.uk>.* Terence Conran's vibrant gastronomic monument to Soho's glamorous people can be both intimidating and exciting. The food is Spanish, with an extensive tapas menu, and there's a wide range of sherries (including sherry cocktails).

Mildred's £–££ *45 Lexington Street, W1, tel: 020 7494 1634; <www.mildreds.co.uk>.* Imaginative vegetarian cooking served in retro, café-style surroundings. Vegan options are also available.

Pizza Express £–££ *10 Dean Street, W1, tel: 020 7437 9595; <www.pizzaexpress.co.uk>.* This branch of this civilised pizza chain is a respected venue on the jazz music circuit. Tasty garlic dough balls and pizza with quirky toppings.

Randall & Aubin ££–£££ *16 Brewer Street, W1, tel: 020 7287 4447; <www.randallandaubin.co.uk>.* Named after the old delicatessen that inhabited this spot from 1904 to the late 1990s, Randall & Aubin is a buzzy, romantic place doing champagne and seafood. Piles of lobster, crabs and oysters greet you as you enter, the music is frenetic and the tables close to each other. Lots of fun.

Wong Kei £ *41–3 Wardour Street, W1, tel: 020 7437 8408.* Infamous for its surly service, this ever-popular Chinatown institution serves food to fill a hole rather than inspire gasps of culinary delight.

Zilli Fish £££ *36–40 Brewer Street, W1, tel: 020 7734 8649; <www.zillialdo.com>.* Buzzy but relaxed, Zilli's does fresh, delicate fish dishes. Try the lobster ravioli, monkfish teriaki or, for those with more traditional tastes, beer-battered cod with fat chips.

THE SOUTH BANK

Anchor Bankside £–££ *34 Park Street, SE1, tel: 020 7407 1577.* This 18th-century riverside pub has higgledy-piggledy rooms with oak beams and a minstrels' gallery. There has been a pub on this site for 1,000 years; Samuel Johnson was a regular.

Cantina Vinopolis £££ *1 Bank End, SE1, tel: 020 7940 8333; <www.cantinavinopolis.com>.* Not surprisingly the restaurant in London's only wine museum has a stunning wine list, with over 100 choices. The food is good, and the soaring cathedral-style arches of pale, polished brick are impressive.

The Fire Station ££ *150 Waterloo Rd, SE1, tel: 020 7620 2226.* Huge portions and a changing menu with a Modern British slant are the pull at this trendy restaurant in a converted fire station right by Waterloo. The only downside is that the bar at the front is noisy.

Fish! ££ *Cathedral Street, close to Borough Market, SE1, tel: 020 7407 3803.* Located in the shadow of Southwark Cathedral – much to the annoyance of the clergy there – this all-glass restaurant serves a great range of fresh and simple dishes. Fish and chips also available.

George Inn £ *77 Borough High Street, SE1; <www.nationaltrust. org.uk>, tel: 020 7407 2056.* Dating from the 17th century, London's only surviving galleried coaching inn is now National Trust-protected. The lunches are basic pub fare such as fish and chips, bangers and mash, soup and chunky sandwiches. The large courtyard with lots of seating is a big draw in summer.

Mesón Don Felipe ££ *53 The Cut, SE1, tel: 020 7928 3237.* This tapas bar has a lively atmosphere and great food. Tables near the door can get bumped by people coming and going, so sit at the counter or towards the back of the room for comfort. A guitarist performs from a raised alcove.

Oxo Tower ££££ *Oxo Wharf, Barge House Street, SE1, tel: 020 7803 3888; <www.harveynichols.com>.* Brasserie and restaurant run by Harvey Nichols combining a chic atmosphere with delicious modern European cuisine and stunning river views. Wonderful cocktails and live music too.

Le Pont de la Tour £££–££££ *Butlers Wharf Building, SE1, tel: 020 7403 8403; <www.conran-restaurants.co.uk>.* Butlers Wharf is Terence Conran land, *par excellence*, and the chic Pont de la Tour restaurant does fine French food such as Millefeuille of Devon crab, cucumber and Sevruga caviar buttersauce. The less formal Bar & Grill downstairs has a Thameside terrace and specialises in seafood.

Tas Pide ££ *20–22 New Globe Walk, SE1, tel: 020 7928 3300; <www.tasrestaurant.com>.* This is one of a small chain of excellent Turkish restaurants, with other branches on The Cut and Borough High Street (both also SE1). Choose from a varied menu of mezze, meat and fish and expect generous portions. Good for vegetarians.

Tate Modern Restaurant 7 £££ *Level 7, Bankside, SE1, tel: 020 7887 8888; <www.tate.org.uk>.* The modern European food, the views and arty, good-looking crowd make dining on the top floor of London's trendiest national institution lots of fun.

WESTMINSTER

The Portrait £££ *National Portrait Gallery, St Martin's Place, WC2, tel: 020 7312 2490; <www.searcys.co.uk>.* When it comes to location, few can beat the National Portrait Gallery's top-floor restaurant with its wonderful views of Trafalgar Square, Big Ben and the London Eye. Above-average gallery food.

Tate Britain Restaurant £££ *Tate Britain, Millbank, SW1, tel: 020 7887 8825; <www.tate.org.uk>.* Beautifully decorated with Rex Whistler's mural, *The Expedition in Pursuit of Rare Meats*, this fine restaurant in the basement of the gallery serves modern European food and has an excellent wine list. Lunch is served from 11.30am to 4pm every day, with afternoon tea from 3.30–5pm.

INDEX

Berlitz pocket guide

London

Eighth Edition 2008

Written by Lesley Logan
Updated by Anna Tyler and
Catherine Dreghorn
Edited by Anna Tyler
Series Editor: Tony Halliday

Photography credits
Natasha Babaian 6; Bridgeman Art Library 14, 18; Jay Fechtman 22, 31; Glyn Genin 20, 27, 35, 42, 56; Tony Halliday 62; Britta Jaschinski 47, 83, 101; LCP 13, 16; Michael Macaroon 64; RBG Kew 89; Sarah Sweeney 48; Science and Society Picture Library 75; Tate London 33; Bill Varie/Corbis 44; Victoria and Albert Museum 73; Visit London Images 8, 9, 10, 11, 24, 25, 28, 30, 34, 37, 38, 39, 41, 45, 50, 53, 55, 57, 58, 61, 67, 68, 70, 71, 76, 78, 81, 84, 86, 90, 93, 94, 95, 97, 98, 100, 102, 104.

Cover picture: Travelpix Ltd/Getty Images

Every effort has been made to provide accurate information in this publication, but changes are inevitable. The publisher cannot be responsible for any resulting loss, inconvenience or injury.

Contact us

At Berlitz we strive to keep our guides as accurate and up to date as possible, but if you find anything that has changed, or if you have any suggestions on ways to improve this guide, then we would be delighted to hear from you.

Berlitz Publishing, PO Box 7910,
London SE1 1WE, England.
fax: (44) 20 7403 0290
email: berlitz@apaguide.co.uk
www.berlitzpublishing.com